AI FOR DEATH AND DYING

AI FOR EVERYTHING

Artificial intelligence (AI) is all around us. From driverless cars to game-winning computers to fraud protection, AI is already involved in many aspects of life, and its impact will only continue to grow in the future. Many of the world's most valuable companies are investing heavily in AI research and development, and not a day goes by without news of cutting-edge breakthroughs in AI and robotics.

The *AI for Everything* series will explore the role of AI in contemporary life, from cars and aircraft to medicine, education, fashion and beyond. Concise and accessible, each book is written by an expert in the field and will bring the study and reality of AI to a broad readership including interested professionals, students, researchers and lay readers.

AI for Immunology
Louis J. Catania

AI for Cars
Hanky Sjafrie & Josep Aulinas

AI for Digital Warfare
Niklas Hageback & Daniel Hedblom

AI for Art
Niklas Hageback & Daniel Hedblom

AI for Death and Dying
Maggi Savin-Baden

AI for Radiology
Oge Marques

AI for Games
Ian Millington

AI for School Teachers
Rose Luckin & Karine George

AI for Learners
Carmel Kent, Benedict du Boulay & Rose Luckin

AI for Social Justice
Alan Dix and Clara Crivellaro

For more information about this series please visit:
https://www.routledge.com/AI-for-Everything/book-series/AIFE

AI FOR DEATH AND DYING

MAGGI SAVIN-BADEN

CRC Press
Taylor & Francis Group
Boca Raton London New York

CRC Press is an imprint of the
Taylor & Francis Group, an **informa** business

First edition published 2022
by CRC Press
6000 Broken Sound Parkway NW, Suite 300, Boca Raton, FL 33487-2742

and by CRC Press
2 Park Square, Milton Park, Abingdon, Oxon, OX14 4RN

CRC Press is an imprint of Taylor & Francis Group, LLC

The right of Maggi Savin-Baden to be identified as author of this work has been asserted by him in accordance with sections 77 and 78 of the Copyright, Designs and Patents Act 1988.

ISBN: 9780367622442 (hbk)
ISBN: 9780367613174 (pbk)
ISBN: 9781003108504 (ebk)

Typeset in Berling
by codeMantra

What we call the beginning is often the end. And to make an end is to make a beginning. The end is where we start from.

Eliot (1942)

To my Godfather, John Isaac.

With thanks for your years of love, prayer and support, I am forever grateful.

CONTENTS

LIST OF FIGURES

LIST OF TABLES

PERMISSIONS

Thanks are due to Jane Wallace who provided the image and permission for the use of the Refind Artefact in Chapter 6.

ACKNOWLEDGEMENTS

This book has been a challenge to create, as understandings of artificial intelligence have been constantly on the move in these liquid times.

I am grateful to Randi Cohen at Taylor & Francis Group who had the idea for this book and has been so supportive in seeing it through. I am also deeply thankful to my husband John who has supported the editing process, and in a home of fun, busyness and chaos are always there to steady the buffs. Any mistakes and errors are mine.

AUTHOR

Maggi Savin-Baden is Professor of Higher Education Research at the University of Worcester, UK and has researched and evaluated staff and student experience of learning for over 20 years and gained funding in this area (Leverhulme Trust, JISC, Higher Education Academy, MoD). She has a strong publication record of over 60 research publications and 19 books which reflect her research interests in the impact of innovative learning, digital fluency, cyber-influence, virtual humans, qualitative research methods, and problem-based learning. In her spare time, she runs, bakes, climbs, does triathlons and has recently taken up wild swimming.

INTRODUCTION

The subject of death and dying is a difficult one, and it is an area that I have been both troubled by and fascinated with since working in the field of oncology in the 1980s. Many years later when working on research projects creating life coaches and virtual humans, I began to link the two areas together. The result was an increasing interest in the possibility for creating a digital immortal. Trying out apps and working with the company Daden Ltd to create a copy of myself continued to fuel my interest in this area. More recently, links with those working in machine learning and artificial intelligence prompted me to realize that an overview of artificial intelligence, death and dying was needed. This book begins the process by providing such an overview in an area where much development is still needed. It begins with Chapter 1 which sets artificial intelligence in the context of current conceptions and defines five different types as the basis for understanding how in later chapters artificial intelligence is seen and used in relation to death and dying. Chapter 2 then explores the portrayal of death and dying in a digital age and some of the new forms of mourning that have emerged in response to death in a digital age.

Chapter 3 explores what it means to memorialize in ethical ways as well as examining the new area of the ethics relating to the creation of robots and digital immortals. The later section of this chapter examines new rituals and practices such as hypermourning and the rise of death goods. The exploration of new practices then leads into Chapter 4, which presents different forms of digital legacy and explores the challenges of managing these as well as the further areas of ownership, security and privacy. The final part of this chapter offers an overview of the death tech industry and discusses the implications of this wide-ranging and often covert industry on people's lives.

Few texts to date have considered religious perspectives in relation to artificial intelligence, death and dying. Chapter 5 begins by exploring the meaning of death. It continues by exploring religious engagement with artificial intelligence, then examines theologies and death and finally presents perspectives on death and artificial intelligence in relation to six different belief systems, namely Christian, Humanist, Sikhism, Buddhism, Hinduism and Islam. The advent of the digital has, it is argued here, enabled the creation of new spaces for the narration of death, both before and after it happens. Chapter 6 explores the idea of pre-death bereavement forms of digital loss and grief, and then explores new digital practices and rituals associated with loss and bereavement.

The final two chapters of this book consider areas that are in development or need to be created in the future. Chapter 7 focuses on the use of artificial intelligence to construct a variety of bots and beings. It begins by locating digital afterlife in relation to symbolic immortality and explains current perceptions of digital afterlife. The final section of this chapter discusses the ethical implications of using a griefbot and creating and developing a digital immortal. Chapter 8 begins by reflecting on the current position of artificial intelligence, death and dying.

It then maps out the way in which different types of artificial intelligence are being or could be used in relation to death and dying and links these to recent relevant research. It is evident that boundaries remain unclear in this area and that the concept of postdigital humans needs to be considered in more depth in relation to death and dying. It also argues that artificial intelligence continues to be a complex and ambiguous area so that research and practice related to its use in this area is in need of considerable development.

This is a book that covers a broad range of literature, research and issues at a time when artificial intelligence itself remains inchoate and messy. Meanwhile, death and dying spaces are perhaps more online than offline, resulting in new and different ways of managing death and dealing with memorialization and mourning.

1

WHAT IS ARTIFICIAL INTELLIGENCE?

INTRODUCTION

This chapter begins by setting artificial intelligence in the context of current conceptions as it is most notable that the idea of artificial intelligence tends to prompt extreme views as well the creation of false hope and concerns. It then examines the various forms of artificial intelligence by defining five different types as the basis for understanding how in later chapters artificial intelligence is seen and used in relation to death and dying. The final section of the chapter suggests that there are a number of challenges raised by the diverse types of artificial intelligence and concludes that automated decision-making is probably more of a concern in the current climate that artificial intelligence.

PORTRAYAL AND PERCEPTIONS OF ARTIFICIAL INTELLIGENCE

Artificial intelligence (AI) is often thought of as robots or thinking machines. In marketing, it is seen as a programme or algorithm often based on machine-learning principles, yet the complexity and diversity of AI is much broader than this. Consequently, AI can be grouped broadly into three main types: first, deep AI which involves creating virtual humans and digital immortals with sentience, the ability to feel, perceive, or experience; second, pragmatic AI where machines are used for tasks such as mining large data sets, or automating complex or risky tasks; and third, marketing AI where companies use algorithms to *anticipate the customer's next move and improve the customer journey.* Often when artificial intelligence (AI) is spoken about in the 21st century, the perspectives that many people have gained are from information presented by media and film. Examples of these are provided in Table 1.1. Furthermore, Recchia (2020) analysed a data set of over 100,000 film subtitles and identified control (or loss of it) as a recurring motif in films about artificial intelligence, which tends to reflect broad public opinion about AI in general (Burden & Savin-Baden, 2019).

Recently, there have been considerable improvements to AI such as better text-to-speech, improved speech recognition and high-quality avatars. Other stances towards AI tend to be much more technical and are based on assumptions about the possibilities for uploading the brain or alternatively using algorithms to predict behaviour and shopping patterns. Frude and Jandric (2015) argue that the real shift in AI will occur when interaction between humans and AI is cumulative. This will result in long-term relationships with the person trusting the machine and in turn the machine adapting to appreciate the person's preferences. However, it is important to note that media and press reports still tend to imply that AI is more developed than it actually is, and it is important to be able to distinguish between clever algorithms, some form of well-developed virtual human and the possibility of creating a virtual persona with sentience some time in the next 40 years.

Table 1.1 Artificial Intelligence in Films and Media

Character	Film/Media (Date Order)	Notion of AI	Difficulty
Hal	*2001: A Space Odyssey* (Kubrick & Clarke, 1968)	Hal controls a spaceship, and prioritizes the mission over the crew	Setting goals for an AI that do not have unintended consequences
Replicants	*Blade Runner* (Deeley & Scott, 1982)	Androids that go rogue, and how to spot them	It is not clear if a replicant knows that it is a replicant.
Data	*Star Trek* (Berman, 1995)	Sentient android as crew mate	Does it have real emotions? Is it too artificial?
Nelson	*The Red Men* (De Abaitua, 2009)	Creating a virtual town of people in order to model human behaviour.	What happens if the computer starts modelling the wrong things – like WW1?
Zoe	*Caprica* (Aubuchon & Moore, 2010)	Making a copy of oneself – and how that copy feels when the creator dies prematurely. Building the copy from digital traces. The importance of a virtual world as 'home'.	The need for a body (Cylons). Is there enough information in the digital traces?

(Continued)

Table 1.1 Artificial Intelligence in Films and Media (*Continued*)

Character	Film/Media (Date Order)	Notion of AI	Difficulty
Ash	Be Right Back (Brooker & Harris, 2013).	The character Ash is built on the basis of his social media profile	It is implied that AI beings can/will have highly advanced emotional responses and empathy.
Ava	Ex Machina (Macdonald & Garland, 2015)	That it is possible to create a true copy of human intelligence	The question of whether a female robot is considered to have human-like intelligence is left to the judgement of a non-expert man selected based on the fact that he will be sexually attracted to her.
Will	Transcendence (Kosove et al., (2014)	Will is shot, and his wife uploads his consciousness into a quantum computer	It presents the idea of a superhuman AI being who transcends the laws of physics
Leila	Kiss Me First (Moggach, 2014)	That massively multiplayer online role-playing games can influence real-world characters so that the real and the fictional activities collide	The person who is killed in real life is still living in the here and now of the game, acting in similar ways as their real-life persona

(*Continued*)

Table 1.1 Artificial Intelligence in Films and Media (*Continued*)

Character	Film/Media (Date Order)	Notion of AI	Difficulty
Ultron	Avengers: Age of Ultron Feige and Whedon (2015)	AI can be used to create a complete copy of a human, but more intelligent.	Ultron is sentient rather than being created as digital immortal personas of other people
Daughter	C4 Humans (Vincent & Brackley, 2015)	A scientist tries to recreate a copy of her dead daughter	There does not seem to be enough information or sophistication to keep it stable
Synths	C4 Humans (Vincent & Brackley, 2015)	Creating worker androids, but then endowing some of them with sentience	The right for the sentient synths to procreate. Whether it is ethical to uplift non-sentient synths.
Girlfriend	Blade Runner 2049 (Kosove & Villeneuve 2017)	AI as a virtual friend/girlfriend.	Limited agency when not needed. Overlaying with a physical sex worker.

(*Continued*)

Table 1.1 Artificial Intelligence in Films and Media (*Continued*)

Character	Film/Media (Date Order)	Notion of AI	Difficulty
Rachel	The After wife (Hunter, 2018)	Rachel (the AI) is created by human Rachel before she dies and without any knowledge or consent from her family	This book raises ethical concerns about not only the rights of the robot, but also about whether family should be consulted pre-death about the creation of a copy
Imagos	Memory of Empire (Martine, 2019)	Creating a copy of your predecessor in a post that exists alongside you in your body as a computer, plugged into your central nervous system	What happens if it overloads or cooks the brain? It is not clear what agency it will be given over the physical body
Daughter	Devs (Garland, 2020)	A dot com billionaire tries to recreate his dead daughter	More by modelling and an assumption of predetermination.

TYPES OF ARTIFICIAL INTELLIGENCE

The early days of research into AI focused on creating computer programmes that could 'understand' and manipulate symbols in order to reason; this was termed symbolic AI. Other forms are embodied AI and enactive AI. Embodied AI is where software is imported into a physical (robotic) body and exploring how that body fits into real-world environments and thus is based on the idea of embodied cognition – the view that intelligence is as much a part of the body as the brain. Enactive AI is seen as a form of AI that refines and complements embodied AI because it has a focus on the self-identity of the robot or virtual human, so that meaning is created by the interaction of the robot with the environment (Froese & Ziemke, 2009). There is also often confusion between AI and augmented intelligence. Augmented intelligence describes either using a computer that is external to the human to help the human with mental tasks or inking computing capability directly into the brain in order to enhance the brain's processing power or memory. The focus here is broadly on the use of AI to help humans with a task, but it also extends to areas such as embodiment and post-digital humans, as these areas have direct impact on the relationship between AI and death and dying. However, whilst AI can be identified through terms such as deep, pragmatic, marketing, embodied or enactive AI, it can also be categorized in terms of its impact and effect. This section positions AI as something that includes a range of concepts from algorithms to posthumanism.

ALGORITHMS AND MACHINE LEARNING

Simple algorithms are used to create a series of steps to undertake a task which in general is straightforward and predictable. These kinds of algorithms often appear sophisticated but in general are not so and cannot really be classed as AI. An example would be Facebook algorithms designed to advertise to individuals, based on their browsing and shopping history. Complex algorithms are often the ones that are being referred to when AI is being discussed and include areas such as machine learning, deep learning, neural networks, Bayesian networks and fuzzy logic. Machine learning is defined here as a computer system that can learn to make decisions based on the examination of past inputs and results, so that its future decisions optimize some parameters – such as facial recognition. However, complex algorithms are often used as shorthand term for AI, when in fact AI is much broader and more complex than this.

ROBOTICS

Robotics is an area that is often confused with artificial intelligence. Robotics is the creation of physical robots, ones that are programmed to carry out a series of actions autonomously, or semi-autonomously. One example was when, in the autumn of 2017, Sophia, a humanoid robot, gave a speech at the United Nations. Other examples include vacuum cleaners, toys, drones, NASA's Robonaut, the humanoid and devices such as the robotic exoskeletons that can be used to enable a paralyzed person to walk again.

Mori's concept of the 'uncanny valley' (Mori, 1970) relates to how objects which are almost, but not quite, human create more of a sense of unease than those which are decidedly not human. Mori identified that, when considering artificial human forms, humans tolerated industrial robots but did not particularly respond to them emotionally. Humans show more affinity and empathy for toy robots and good quality (anime and manga style) human-like but still visually artificial toys. In the world of film, the sense of the uncanny often occurs when audience response is misread. For example, after the film Cats (Hayward et al., 2019) was released, producers were puzzled as to why the audiences disliked it so much. Founder of consumer science company CrowdCat,

Richard Summers, explains, 'because the high quality special effects made the cast look halfway between cats and humans, this created sexual and social anxiety for the audience, in the main it was the lack of genitalia that audiences found so unsettling' (personal communication February 2021). However, research also suggests that people find robots wearing clothes and with fake skin as being creepy, but what is clear is that people will interact with avatars and chatbots 'as if' they were human (Burden & Savin-Baden, 2019). Yet Borenstein and Arkin (2016) argue that the main issues that need to be considered are affective attachment, responsiveness and the extent and duration of the proximity between the human and the robot.

EMBODIMENT

Embodiment has been discussed extensively in education and computer science. For example, the creation and use of avatars in educational games and virtual worlds have introduced questions about the sense of being embodied, the relationship with the avatar and the challenge of identity construction. In AI, embodiment is seen less about the relationship between what it means to be human and AI construction, and more about the concept of embodiment – the importance of a person having a 'physical' sense of self; embodiment is thus seen as a vital part of consciousness. Most of the discussion about situatedness and embodiment has been in the context of AI and physical robots. One of the drivers for an embodied and situated approach to AI was to move away from the artificial and the virtual to the real, everyday, physical environment so that the AI could learn to deal with the clutter and chaos of the real world. However, virtual worlds offer the opportunity to explore how the ideas of embodiment and situatedness could apply to virtual humans in virtual worlds. These 3D digital multi-user virtual environments (MUVEs) are used by humans (through their avatars) for a whole variety of business, recreational and academic purposes. The main challenge that could be made to virtual humans, in the form of an avatar in a virtual world, being 'embodied' is that unlike an AI driving a physical robot, they have no physical bodies – they literally have no physical embodiment. An early study by Benford et al. (1995) explored user embodiment on collaborative virtual environments. The purpose of the study was to provide users with what researchers considered to be appropriate representative body images. The underlying argument here is that because in real life, bodies provide continuous information, feedback and means of communication, embodiment in virtual environments should be the same, so that participants can represent themselves as accurately as possible. The issues of embodiment are also seen in experiments relating to haptics: the use of technology that creates a sense of touch such as vibration or movement in order to enhance visual engagement, in the virtual worlds. Examples of this include response feedback through gloves, using retinal projection, and employing photorealism in order to use one's real-life face on one's avatar. Other areas of experiment include motion capture where sensors on clothing are used in order to link real-world movement with inworld movement for activities such as in-world performance and theatre.

VIRTUAL HUMANS

It is evident from the literature that the label virtual humans tend to be used as an overarching one that include other terms such as Chatbots, Conversational Agents and Pedagogical Agents (Table 1.2).

Virtual humans are perceived to be human-like characters on a computer screen with embodied life-like behaviours which may include speech, emotions, locomotion, gestures and movements of the head, eyes or other parts of the body.

Table 1.2 Types of Virtual Humans

	Definition	Example
Autonomous agent	A software programme which operates autonomously according to a particular set of rules. Sometimes used synonymously with chatbots.	Stock trading (Subramanian, et al., 2006)
Avatar	The bodily manifestation of one's self or a virtual human in the context of a 3D virtual world, or even as a 2D image within a text-chat system.	A basic one can be created at http://doppelme.com/create/, but avatars are more often using in gaming.
Chatbot	A software programme that attempts to mimic human conversation when communicating with another (usually human) user.	Hello Barbie (Rhodan, 2015) allows children to have pseudoconversations with a doll.
Conversational agent	Virtual humans whose task is to provide a conversational interface to a particular application, for tasks ranging from making travel bookings to interrogating marketing data.	Shopping assistants from H&M or Sephora
Pedagogical agent	A virtual human used for educational purposes. The function of pedagogical agents is to aid learners during the learning process. These agents aim to support learners by providing easier access to relevant information and to improve motivation	Improving learner motivation (for example, Schroeder & Adesope, 2014).

(*Continued*)

Table 1.2 Types of Virtual Humans (*Continued*)

	Definition	Example
Virtual life coach	A virtual human who acts as a mentor and provides guidance, rather than merely simple access to information.	Mobile apps such as Wysa (https://www.wysa.io/) and Woebot (https://woebot.io/).
Virtual persona	A model of a single individual, with their personality traits, (only) the knowledge and experience that they have gained or have heard of, and with a subjective and possibly flawed view of reality.	An example of the creation of Virtual Barry can be found in Savin-Baden and Burden (2018).

So perhaps useful working definitions, (following Burden & Savin-Baden, 2019) are

- *Virtual humanoids*. Simple virtual humans reflect some of the behaviour, emotion, thinking, autonomy and interaction of a physical human.
- *Virtual humans*. Software programmes which present as human and which may have behaviour, emotion and interaction modelled on physical human capabilities.
- *Virtual sapiens*. Sophisticated virtual humans which achieve similar levels of presentation, behaviour, emotion, interaction, self-awareness and internal narrative to a physical human.

POSTHUMANISM

The development and use of postdigital humans is occurring rapidly, but often in unexpected ways and spaces. Posthumanism seeks to break down binary distinctions between 'human', 'machine' and 'text' and between 'nature' and 'culture'; it also rejects dualisms that are used to define being, such as subject/

object (Hayles, 1999, 2012). Thus, posthumanist theory is used to question the foundational role of 'humanity'. In the late 1990s and early 2000s, ideas about postdigital humans related to the enhancement of humans. For example, in 1998 a set of experiments, known as Project Cyborg, were undertaken by Kevin Warwick who began by having an implant placed into his arm used to control doors, lights and heaters. In 2021, postdigital humans now refer more often to the ways in which humans are seen in relationship, mutually shaping one another, whilst recognizing what is new as well as what is already embedded in our cultures, institutions, political systems and relationships. This prompts consideration of what it means to be a human subject and the extent to which the idea of the human subject is still useful. Postdigital human creation might also include whole brain emulation (Hanson, 2008) whereby brain scan data are translated into software based on the neurons and other key parts of the brain, and the Singularity, the view that there will be a time in the future when technological growth becomes uncontrollable and irreversible. It has been suggested that 2050–2100 might be the time period in which the development of really complex postdigital humans capable of being called virtual sapiens will occur (Burden and Savin-Baden, 2019), but whether active ones will emerge before then is questionable.

CHALLENGES OF ARTIFICIAL INTELLIGENCE

Artificial intelligence is already shaping and reshaping our lives, environments, and relationships with other people. The result is that AI can be referred to as anything from a simple algorithm to a complex virtual persona who has the possibility for future sentience. The challenges of AI largely relate to the fact that many definitions are broad and unclear. Current perspectives tend to focus on the wide parameters between fear and hope, such as AI resulting in loss of work, enslaving humans and making them obsolete, to the hope of AI providing virtual human support to elderly and disabled people, and providing entertainment as well as supporting security and defence systems. The main current challenges are ones of trust, security, realism, public perception, ethics, and race and gender.

TRUST

AI, of whatever sort, has social implications and raises questions about what counts as privacy. Questions need to be considered as to whether it is acceptable to use a webcam to spy on the person who is baby-sitting your child or to film your roommate at university as a joke? Certainly, the current situation with automated decision-making, tracking through apps such as Strava, as well as the use of face recognition in shopping centres, suggests that privacy and trust is something that the public needs to be more aware of.

SECURITY

Enforcing security now carries a huge financial cost and therefore the protection of some areas is favoured over others. The question is what should be left unsecure and what might this mean? Furthermore, it is also important to consider whether there is now really any possibility of privacy or secure identities. It seems our identities can be both stolen or borrowed, as well as even used against us, perhaps not imminently but certainly in our future lives and work.

REALISM

Studies that compared human interviewees with virtual world chatbots (pedagogical agents in non-learning situations) indicate that chatbots and human interviewees were equally successful in collecting information about their participants' real-life backgrounds (Savin-Baden et al., 2013). To date, research into the realism of chatbots has formed both the greater part and the basis of use for many of these technologies. Perhaps what we are really beginning to deal with here is 'augmented existence'. The notion of augmented existence is the idea that it is not just the tagging and integration that is affecting our lives, but the fact that the meta systems themselves become a new means of categorization.

PUBLIC PERCEPTION

There needs to be a way to bridge the gap between the public perceptions of AI – as already mentioned, and the reality of what is currently being called AI. For example, AI is still used as a generic term that includes everything from machine learning, data science and algorithms to the creation of virtual humans. Furthermore, many people are largely unaware of the impact that marketing AI may have, and at the same time others appear to believe that it will possible a virtual human with sentience by 2020. Whilst creating such a virtual human may be something that is unlikely to occur for several decades, it is important to understand the possible consequences beforehand since such a creation will create consequences that will be immense. Even AI that uses simple algorithms is likely to possess the ability to change employment patterns significantly as well as to affect moral and ethical norms.

ETHICS

There are ethical concerns where AI agents are designed to achieve specific purposes such as supporting online shopping, promoting services or goods, or supporting student learning. There are two key ethical issues at hand here. First, there is the issue of whether research participants are aware of who is 'behind the computer' and whether they believe that they are engaging with a human, or with an artificially intelligent technology. This leads to the second ethical issue of participant willingness to disclose information to non-human researchers. A recent study (Savin-Baden & Bhakta, 2019) explored the use of online problem-based learning to examine whether students could detect a covert pedagogical agent within in their small group task. Problem-based learning is a form of learning where students learn the curricular content through problem scenarios rather than subjects or disciplines. Students work in groups or teams to solve or manage these situations, but they are not expected to acquire a predetermined series of 'right answers'. Instead, they are expected to engage with the complex situation presented to them and decide what information they need to learn and what skills they need to gain in order to manage the situation effectively. The findings of the study indicate that fact few students detected the agent; furthermore, many students attributed human characteristics to the pedagogical agent, and some became highly irritated by it. Despite several students being concerned about the pedagogical agent confusing other group members and providing responses that were inappropriate, for one student the pedagogical agent was seen as a useful member of the group. This raises questions about whether higher education institutions are likely to implement the use of hidden pedagogical agents in online and virtual learning environments, and how ethical this is if students are not aware of this change in teaching.

A major ethical consideration is the emergence of digital immortality, (Savin-Baden et al., 2017) now referred to as digital afterlife (Savin-Baden et al., 2017). Digital immortality is the continuation of an active or passive digital presence after death. Whilst society is beginning to grapple with passive digital immortality, for example through Facebook memorialization, even current chatbot technology could create an active presence for the deceased, and the distinction between a person physically alive or dead could cease for most of the people with whom they interact. Quite apart from family, moral and relationship issues, there are also ethical and legal issues that would need to be considered, and protection against exploitation by companies seeking commercial gain, which will be discussed later in Chapter 5.

RACE AND GENDER

Clearly in many of the AI films, gender stereotypes, for instance, are perpetuated by fictional narratives as well as real-life technology. For example, Alexa perpetuates the stereotype of family roles and responsibilities when one advert shows a mother setting-up Alexa in order to provide the father guidance on childcare, thus necessarily assuming that this is a job a man cannot do. The bodily markers that are used to present ourselves in life, clothes, ethnicity, gender and speech may be represented (differently) in virtual spaces, but they also indicate choices about how we wish to be seen or the ways in which we might like to feel differently. However, as Nakamura (2010) suggests, we might be aware that these kinds of media (games and virtual embodiment) create social factions of race and gender, whilst accurate images of gender and cultural realties might be rare. One of the issues about appearance is also that of morphology, particularly in relation to gender, race and ethnicity. Race stereotypes, for example, are reinforced through the images available on sites such as Pixabay and iStock of anthropomorphic robots, which portray a muscular white plastic man often with Caucasian features. Until fairly recently, avatars in virtual worlds have been young, thin and Caucasian. Robertson (2010) has raised questions about the over-feminization of the platforms in relation to the fembots in Japan, and it is also notable that there are very few black virtual humans.

In the context of this book, AI will be discussed predominantly in relation to virtual humans. This is because whilst death-tech sites do use algorithms to advertise their services, the main focus here is on the use and impact of AI pre- and post-death. The portrayal of post-death possibilities in film and media tends to imply that more is possible than is actually the case. However, books such as *The After Wife* (Hunter, 2018) do tackle some of the possible future conundrums such as virtual human rights, perceived sentience as well as loss and bereavement – both of the human and the virtual human.

RESEARCH AND REGULATION

Hern reported that The European Parliament has urged the drafting of a set of regulations to govern the use and creation of robots and artificial intelligence (Hern, 2017). The areas that need to be addressed are suggested to be

- The creation of a European agency for robotics and AI.
- A legal definition of 'smart autonomous robots', with a registration for the most advanced.
- An advisory code of conduct to guide the ethical design, production and use of robots.
- A new reporting structure for companies requiring them to report the contribution of robotics and AI to the economic results of a company for the purpose of taxation and social security contributions
- A mandatory insurance scheme for companies to cover damage caused by their robots.

The report also takes a special interest in the future of autonomous vehicles, such as self-driving cars, but as yet there seems relatively little detail about how this might be implemented or developed or indeed how the relationship between AI and virtual humans might operate.

AUTOMATED DECISION-MAKING

Automated decision-making (ADM) is where the system makes a judgment about what is likely to be relevant in the future. The extent to which this is effective relies on a system's familiarity with users' preferences. An example of prediction through ADM is Amazon and Google, for instance, Cadwalladr reported in The Guardian that

> Google has gone on an unprecedented shopping spree and is in the throes of assembling what looks like the greatest artificial intelligence laboratory on Earth; a laboratory designed to feast upon a resource of a kind that the world has never seen before: truly massive data. Our data. From the minutiae of our lives.
>
> Cadwalladr (2014)

More recently, ADM has been described as algorithmically controlled decisions that may be partly or fully delegated to someone or to an organization who then uses decision-making models to execute an action. In this case, it is the system that is of concern (AlgorithmWatch, 2019). An example of such concerns can be seen in the debates about face recognition and face verification, as discussed in the section below.

PRIVACY THREATS

Whether there can be any kind of real symmetry between people and machines centres on ethical concerns, which is clearly evident in debates about face recognition and face verification. Big Brother Watch, the independent research and campaigning group, exposes and challenges threats to privacy, freedoms, and civil liberties amid technological change in the UK. One of its main campaigns is FaceOff, which challenges the use of automated facial recognition in policing (Big Brother Watch, 2020).

MORALITY AND ETHICS

In the field of machine learning, there has been increasing realization that there needs to be a delineation between different types of ethics: robotics ethics, machine morality and intimacy ethics are all new areas that being examined. For example, Malle (2016) argues that robot ethics needs to examine ethical questions about how humans should design, deploy and treat robots. Machine morality explores issues about what moral capacities a robot or virtual human should have and how these might be implemented. For example, Google Duplex was recently able to book a restaurant table verbally without the other party realizing that they were talking to a computer (Leviathan, 2018). Machine morality also includes issues such as moral agency justification for lethal military robots, the use of mathematical proofs for moral reasoning and intimacy ethics. Intimacy ethics relates to the ways in which engaging with virtual humans can offer people opportunities to connect with something emotionally and feel supported, even loved, without the need to reciprocate.

AUTOMATED DECISION-MAKING OR ARTIFICIAL INTELLIGENCE?

It is clear that much of the discussion about humans and machines in the 2020s should be focusing on automated decision-making (ADM), rather than artificial intelligence. AlgorithmWatch (2019) compiled findings from 12 European countries to examine regulation and systems that have already been implemented. The company recommends that there is a need to see ADM as more than just the use of technology. Instead, the company argues that the focus should be on the way the technology is developed and deployed and by whom. Section 49 of General Data Protection Regulation (GDPR) states the right not to be subject to automated decision-making in the following way:

A controller may not take a significant decision based solely on automated processing unless that decision is required or authorised by law.

A decision is a "significant decision" for the purpose of this section if, in relation to a data subject, it—

(a) produces an adverse legal effect concerning the data subject, or

(b) significantly affects the data subject.

Data Protection Act (2018).

AlgorithmWatch argues that this section of the Act is limited as some ADM systems cannot be regulated just by data protection, such as predictive policing. This is the use of software that applies statistical data to guide decision-making. In practice, this means analysing statistical historic data to predict increased risk of criminal activity in given geographic areas. Thus, AlgorithmWatch suggests that it is vital to ensure that stakeholders are involved in the design of criteria and that decisions and evaluations about ADM include organizations – such as Big Brother Watch. As yet it is not clear what the extent of the use of ADM is in areas of death and bereavement, although the death-tech industry continues to grow.

CONCLUSION

This chapter has explored AI from the broad stance of film and media portrayal to concerns about ADM. Artificial intelligence continues to be a confusing ill-defined realm, covering areas from algorithms, marketing and machine learning to virtual human and posthumanism. What is clear is that AI is certainly an area that will have an impact on those using it to remember loved ones and to create pre- and post-death virtual humans. Concerns about death and dying in the digital age will be explored further in Chapter 2

2

DEATH AND DYING IN THE DIGITAL AGE

INTRODUCTION

This chapter begins by exploring the portrayal of death and dying in a digital age. It suggests that media representations of death have resulted in a distancing from the realities of death and a sense of sanitization towards it. This chapter then explores media discourses of death and the relationship between artificial intelligence and death. The next section examines models of grief in the context of artificial intelligence and suggests that a more recent model of grief – orientation towards network grief, is possibly the most useful approach to date. The final section explores some of the new forms of mourning that have emerged in response to death in a digital age.

DEATH IN THE DIGITAL AGE

Death and dying in the 21st century are managed by religion, society, business and the media. Dying is invariably handled outside the home and the process of dying spoken of in hushed tones or not at all. Death is administered through varied practices by funeral directors designed to sanitize death and relieve the family of the burden of death, smoothing the initial shock of bereavement. Most religious practices, as will be discussed in Chapter 5, in the main are designed to help loved ones confront death in realistic ways, but media portrayal of death continues to be problematic as well as an area of fasciation. For example, media increasingly shapes how death is perceived and affects how death is dealt with publicly, organizationally and behaviourally. Table 2.1 presents a few of the diverse ways that death is portrayed – from death photography to the voyeurism associated with death.

The human concern and fascination with death appears to have changed relatively little over the centuries. This is seen not only in the media but also in the desire to preserve the dead through burial, artefact and memorialization. For example, in the Christian tradition the use of embalming stemmed from a medieval belief that preservation of the body indicated a sign of favour from God. In other religions, grave goods are buried with the body, such as personal possessions, food and drink designed to either ease the deceased's journey into the afterlife or provide them with what was needed in the afterlife. Memorialization ranges from roadside flowers to Facebook memorial pages as well as the creation of post-death avatars. However, what is pertinent here are the shifts and new perspectives on the discourses surrounding different forms of death.

DISCOURSES OF DEATH

Whilst death is a difficult topic face to face, and knowing what to say to a bereaved person can be uncomfortable, there is a strong new sense of how death should be managed as portrayed through media stories. Clarke (2006) examined the portrayal of death by examining the highest circulating mass media magazine available in Canada and the USA. Her findings indicate that there was a perception that death should be 'within our control' (p. 157) and that it should be a choice. Clarke presents five portrayals of death discourses that emerged from her study.

Table 2.1 Portrayal of Death in the Media

Media	Example	Explanation
Death photography	Hanging of Saddam Hussein	Visual representation used in ways to legitimize journalists' authority as truth tellers
Death as spectacle	Six Feet Under (Ball, 2001–2005)	A US television series that explores death from personal, philosophical and religious perspectives but also suggests that death is a public spectacle
Death as performance	Hamlet (Shakespeare, 1609/2008)	Death is a central theme performed off stage and onstage, and portrayal as both a performance and as a concept with dark humour and irony
Death as denial	Fearless (Weinstein et al., 1993)	A film in which the main character survives a near-death experience and then undertakes action to seek to defy death
Death games	Call of Duty (2003–2020)	A first-person shooter game based on World War II, The Cold War and futuristic worlds. Although most of the games are designed to challenge and make the player uncomfortable, there is a likelihood that the players become anesthetized to the shooting and ravages of war over time
Death as voyeurism	My Last Words (Hakola, 2013)	A reality show that focuses on death and dying. It is seen by some people as sensationalizing death and encouraging voyeurism

EUTHANASIA

Clarke found that media accounts of euthanasia included stories about keeping people alive despite them being in a coma, the decision of people to abort the child due to a genetic disorder and the compassionate killing of a severely disabled child by her father. What is complex in the ongoing debates about euthanasia is the issues of informed consent and the different types of euthanasia. However, what is clear is that to date, there is little, if anything, that deals with the concept of digital euthanasia – the self-killing of one's data before death or one's pre-death avatar.

SUICIDE

Clarke (2006) described stories of suicide bombers and those who want to broadcast their death to show the importance of being able to choose the time, place and guest list as well as the method of dying. There were also a considerable number of articles reporting celebrity suicide. Films such as Eye in the Sky (2015) explore the ethics and complexity of government responsibility in suicide bombing as well as the media portrayal of it.

THE RIGHT TO DIE MOVEMENT

Magazines reported several stories of medically assisted suicide, the role of medicine in assisting death as well as articles about controversies surrounding the right to die movement.

Interestingly in the context of the right to die movement, the notion of suffering is central. In a study by Karsosho et al. (2016), proponents of physician-assisted dying were interviewed in order to explore the notion of suffering and the role of medicine at the end of life within the context of a decriminalization and legalization debate. The article draws on Carter v. Canada, the court case that decriminalized physician-assisted dying in Canada in 2015 (Karsoho, 2015). The findings indicate the different ways proponents construct relationships between suffering, mainstream curative medicine, palliative care and assisted dying. The authors suggest that the articulation of suffering with the role of medicine at the end of life should be understood as a discourse through which one configuration of end-of-life care comes to be accepted and another rejected, a discourse that ultimately does not challenge, but makes productive use of the larger framework of the medicalization of dying.

MURDER

There were a different number of stories about different types of murder from jilted husbands killing their wives to the murder of gay men. It is notable that in the 2020s, whether in magazines or television, the general public are perceived to have increased fascination with murder compared with former years, as exemplified by the rise in TV dramas in this area. Interestingly, a study by Jones (2020) suggests that murder committed in the context of anger and jealousy was brought about through social media from one person to the next. The study argues that social media allows people to not take responsibility for their words and actions.

STRATEGIES FOR LIVING LONGER

The articles presented by Clarke on living longer focus on several issues such as physical exercise, products and clinics that can help to prevent ageing. Other articles by Clarke also suggest it is possible to lengthen life and discuss general possibilities for anti-ageing intervention. Clarke notes that media portrayal of death in magazines suggests that death is

Often a matter of individual freedom, the result of personal preference and thus potentially or actually under control. People can elect to suicide to extend their lives, to use euthanasia as they will. Death is not random, unwelcome or to be feared. It is not portrayed in the context of prevention, suffering, palliation or community supports. The links between economic, ethnic and other forms of inequality and death rates are ignored.

Clarke (2006: 162), italics in original

What is particularly interesting about Clarke's study is the indication that the media focus for managing death is through medicine rather than artificial intelligence technology. Thus, the idea of 'medicide', that is, death through medical intervention, suggests that the societal view is that death needs to be chosen and managed by the individual, whilst still alive. What is also of interest is that Clarke notes the absence in media portrayal of death of

- Discussion of poverty violence, racism inequality and international conflict
- Death occurring naturally amidst family and friends
- Death described as a positive end of life journey
- The role of religion in death.

These findings illustrate that media portrayal of death obfuscates the complexities and pain of death and loss, resulting in a sense that individuals have the right to control their own death on their own terms. This perhaps also reflects the desire to use artificial intelligence to manage death through the creation of post-death avatars.

DEATH AND ARTIFICIAL INTELLIGENCE

The recent trilogy by Shusterman begins with the novel Scythe (Shusterman, 2016). Here, we are presented with a world managed by a sentient artificially intelligent being, the Thunderhead who watches and controls the world, but does not control death. The world has become overpopulated because death is always curable, except by fire, so in order to manage the population, human scythes are a self-appointed group who 'glean' humans in order to manage the population.

The sentient Thunderhead, whilst seeming not to interfere, does manipulate humans to a degree to try to manage the more evil scythes. Whilst this story might seem worlds away from the 21st century, humanity can and does manage death but in discrete and hidden ways through voluntary euthanasia and voluntary suicide.

To date, in-depth discussion and research into death and AI are relatively uncommon. Many of the debates relate to the possibility and reliability of death prediction through AI such as the Death Date Calculator Clock Timer. This is a free app that calculates when you will die and gives Free Life Predictions and suggestions on the basis of your health, status, height, weight and lifestyle. The app not only calculates your death date but also suggests the solution to extend your remaining life and delay the death. More serious predictions are being used in healthcare such as a new algorithm developed by researchers at Stanford University (Wiederhold, 2019). The algorithm has the ability to predict the time of death within 3–12 months for a hospital inpatient. The process claims to be >90% accurate, and thus, hospital admission decisions in the future could be made on the basis of screening health records with artificial intelligence to determine the patient's need for palliative care before death. There are similar studies exploring the use of algorithms in areas such as heart disease and suicide prevention. For example, the healthcare provider Geisinger US used an AI system to examine 1.77 million electrocardiogram (ECG) results from nearly 400,000 people to predict who was at a higher risk of dying within the next year (Lu, 2019).

Whilst artificial intelligence is being used to predict death, it is also being used to map the life of the deceased in cyberspace. The possibilities range from memorialization pages provided by funeral directors, and other sites such as MyWishes, which can be used to create pre- and post-death avatars. This death tech industry is growing and will be presented and discussed further in Chapter 4. However, it is useful at this point to discuss the presence of the dead in cyberspace.

THE DEAD IN CYBERSPACE

Whilst graveyards are clearly sites of absence, in cyberspace there is sense or a belief that the dead are present. For example, Nansen et al. (2015) coined the term the restless dead to refer to the ways in which forms of digital commemoration are resulting in cultural shifts towards a restless posthumous existence. It is not that the dead themselves are perceived to be restless but that there is a shift away from the idea of death as being sleep or rest. Instead, the dead are eternally present in cyberspace as they materialize through social media and technical capabilities. Such media include living headstones, digitally augmented coffins and commemorative urns embodying the head of the deceased. This ongoing presence tends to create the sense that cyberspace and the dead within it transcend the finality of the death by interrupting the previous limitations of cemeteries, static headstones and biological death. The consequence Kasket suggests is digital persistence. Kasket (2019) argues that online persistence and the ongoing presence of the data of the dead online will lead to more of a globalized, secularized ancestor veneration culture and it is important to recognize the ongoing persistence of the dead online on social media, LinkedIn, Amazon and YouTube.

However, such persistence may be intentional or accidental immortality. Intentional forms of digital immortality creation include transferring all assets both digital and nondigital into a digital legacy, adding to current media memories pre-death, creating a digital immortal (avatar) pre-death and creating a digital immortal that would learn post-death. Most of these forms are likely to be discussed with loved one's pre-death, and therefore, the intentions and use of them are likely to be clear. What is more of a concern is if they have been intentionally created but not shared pre-death. Accidental immortality occurs when media are preserved without the deceased realizing it pre-death. In 2019, Perfect Choice Funerals in the UK undertook a survey and found that the majority of people over 50s are not aware of the memorialization feature of social media profiles. They asked 1,000 people aged 50 and above about their knowledge of social media in relation to mortality. Seventy percent of respondents were not aware that social media accounts could be memorialized. Those who were aware of memorialization online were then asked whether they had personally memorialized someone's profile, and they found that 3% had actually done it themselves, despite 18% saying that they had seen memorialized profiles (Perfect Choice Funerals, 2020). Whilst some people value engaging with the internet and digital media when they are alive, they may believe that part of the leaving, grieving and forgetting process for those left behind means deleting all digital media. This deletionist stance can result in conflict with those who want to preserve all the artefacts of the dead as well as creating the deceased as a digital immortal as well. For preservationists, it is important in terms of ancestry to preserve everything from online spaces. Differences in familial stances of a change of view post-death are likely to cause conflict and difficulty for the living. However, understanding how people respond to the dead in cyberspace also relates to the ways in which grief is perceived and managed.

MODELS OF GRIEF

Although there has been research and exploration into artificial intelligence and the creation of pre- and post-death avatars (also referred to as digital immortals), the relationship between artificial intelligence and models of grief remains an area that has been studied little. There are a number of models of death and grief ranging from stage models to circular models. Kubler-Ross (1969) argued for five Stages of responses to Death which may not always be experienced in the same order. So, whilst it is often seen as a staged model, it is, in fact, a circular model with reoccurring stages (Figure 2.1).

Although this is presented as a cycle with an apparent ending in acceptance, it is suggested here that there are likely to be stuck places along the way as well as movement back to bargaining and anger. Thus, grief here is a transitional process which has similarities with the phased model suggested by Murray-Parkes (1971). This model considers people's history, experiences to date and in particular their relationship with the deceased; phases will differ in each case according to the relationship with the deceased. These four phases are shock and numbness; yearning and searching; disorientation and disorganization; and reorganization and resolution.

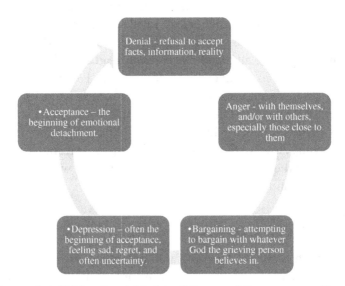

Figure 2.1 Kubler Ross' Model of Stages of Responses to Death presented as a cycle.

It is widely recognized that grief stages apply not only to grief following a bereavement, but also to many other types of loss and trauma, such as amputation and personal reactions to change or life events. In terms of artificial intelligence, these models could be applied to people's responses not only to physical death but also to the notion of second loss. Second loss is the loss experienced due to the deletion of digital remains (Bassett, 2018). The bereaved person is faced with the original loss of the loved one, and the emotional consequences of exposure to their digital legacy, followed by the actual or potential loss of this digital legacy in the future.

These stages have been recognized, adopted and adapted universally in the past. However, during the 1990s different theories of loss and mourning were suggested, which would seem to have greater resonance with the idea of artificial intelligence. These included the following.

DURABLE BIOGRAPHY

Walter (1996) argues that the purpose of grieving is to construct a durable biography that allows survivors to continue to integrate the deceased person into their lives and to find a stable and secure place for them. Walter's work here refers to a durable biography based on the deceased in their physical life, but the possibility for digital afterlife creation means that new forms of durable biographies can be created. Perhaps instead of a durable biography, it will be an 'enduring biography' based on a digital legacy created after death.

CONTINUING BONDS

Throughout most of the 20th century, it was expected that grieving involved a process of letting go, breaking bonds with the deceased. The continuing bonds model was developed by Klass et al. (1996) who argued instead that in fact, the relationship with the deceased changes, rather than breaks. In short, the relationship does not end. It challenged the popular models of grief requiring the bereaved to detach from the deceased. Thus, the model suggests that grief is not a linear process to be worked through which is completed when someone 'moves on'. Instead after death, the relationship is redefined so that some kind of attachment is perceived to be normal. The focus is on a changed relationship, a continuing bond with the deceased, rather than a letting go and moving on. However, recently Klass has remarked that maintaining a connection with the dead is a common aspect of bereavement in all current models of grief which is reflected in the use of digital and social media for this purpose (Klass, 2018). A similar model was proposed by Tonkin (1996) that of Growing around Grief. This model suggests that grief does not necessarily disappear over time, but instead of moving on from grief, people 'grow around it'. Continuing bonds and growing around grief are both models that support the idea of digital afterlife creation through artificial intelligence.

DUAL PROCESS GRIEVING

This model of grieving (Stroebe & Schut, 1999) suggests that there are two categories of stressors affecting bereavement: loss orientation and restoration orientation. Loss orientation refers to the way the bereaved person processes the actual loss. In practice, this means that they oscillate between confronting and avoiding issues connected with grieving. The restoration orientation refers to the secondary consequences of bereavement such as dealing with the world without the deceased person in it. The model also suggests that it is important to take respite from dealing with both of these stressors in order to adapt and cope. However, the dual process model would be interrupted if a post-death digital immortal were to be created. The process of loss could be affected by the continual interaction with the digital immortal and may also prevent the person grieving their loved one by not reengaging with the world.

Whilst these models can be related to the creation of digital afterlife, digital immortals and digital memorialization, a number of concepts and practices around grieving and digital have developed during this century.

ORIENTATION TO NETWORK GRIEF

This is a new model of grief that was developed as a result of a 5-year mixed methods study. Brubaker et al. (2019) sought to understand how people positioned themselves and evaluated their expression of networked grief. What emerged from this study was a new cyclical model of grief pertinent to the digital age. It comprises stances that are dynamic and continuous processes:

- *Encounter.* Here, an individual encounters another's expression of grief on a social networking site, which prompts the dynamic process of orienting to networked grief.
- *Situate.* Once an expression of grief is encountered, the person seeks to locate themselves and the other person in relationship to their understandings of the network structure, for example, whether they are a close friend, family or celebrity. This categorization then affects how they evaluate the expression of grief in terms of emotional content and appropriateness.
- *Evaluate.* The individual evaluates the expression of grief based on the understanding of the network, and by the norms an individual has learned for appropriate behaviour both on Facebook and grief more broadly.
- *Reassess.* Re-evaluation of how the individual and others are situated in the networks, such as realizing someone may have been closer to the deceased than they first

appreciated or that Facebook is too trite space for grief management.

Establish. Orientation. Individuals establish an orientation in relationship to the network so that when they have a sense of the norms and expression of grief, they come to understand their own position within it.

Act. Once an orientation to the network is established, individuals make decision about current future encounters as well as their relationship to the network over time.

LOSS AND MOURNING IN A DIGITAL AGE

Adjusting to loss is a social activity which occurs in the conversations between the living about the dead and between the living and the dead. Klass (2006) suggests that what is central to managing loss is a focus on understanding community, cultural and political narratives of loss. There have been a number of studies that have begun to explore the issues of loss in a digital age, and in particular, the impact of the loss of people's digital remains from social media sites (Bassett, 2018; Kasket, 2019). Yet at the same time, there is also exploration into new practices associated with mourning.

Mourning customs have changed in terms of practices, but not perhaps in terms of behaviours. Mourning behaviours appear to be quite similar to past activities, but what is different is that they occur in different spaces. Such spaces include social media sites and the use of photographs for communication. Wagner (2018) reviewed a range of studies exploring mourning online and highlights that norms are constantly changing and renegotiated by users of social media. A distinction is also made between those who are mourning themselves, and reactions to the mourning of others, highlighting the need to consider the needs of both mourners and the users of social media who are reacting to expressions of grief online. Furthermore, Cann (2014) notes that in some instances, grief rituals online and posting about the deceased are taken away from the families who are the primary mourners. This is because other people usurp this traditional hierarchy since it is not recognized in social media spaces, and often, this privilege and privacy is not protected by other people who knew the deceased. There are new ways of describing mourning from the second death to bandwagon mourning, as explained below.

SOCIAL MEDIA SPACES AND PRESENCING

The most commonly used virtual graveyard spaces in the early 2020s are Facebook and Twitter. The value of these spaces is that they can be accessed from anywhere, have flexible opening times and have permanence and persistence. Digital photographs are often used to communicate life through such practices as presencing. Presencing in the social media context refers to the individual situating them themselves in a place or space (such as at a funeral) and making the occasion known to others through social media by a comment, post, photograph or tweet. Taking photographs has become both an embedded form of presencing in mourning practices and an attempt to communicate grief to a wider social network.

SECOND DEATH

The term 'second death' has become a popular and well-used term when discussing loss in a digital age. The term was coined by Stokes (2015) where he argued people die twice: once when they stop breathing and then again when the last person speaks their name. Thus, my father may die, but second death will not occur until the last member of my family or friends ceases to speak his name. He also suggests that the term 'digital remains' should be used to refer to their digital data and memories, since this, he believes, offers a sense of them having value and status. The idea is that the second death is not a physical death but a social one, and thus, their digital remains reflect the social life of the dead person. However, in terms of digital media Stokes suggests that social death has become more complicated than before the age of the digital. This is because suggest the data of the dead are an 'object of moral obligation', and therefore, these digital remains should not be deleted. Yet remembering the dead differs across people and families, and as studies have shown recently (Bassett, 2018; Kasket, 2019), not everyone believes that digital memories and messages should be preserved after death.

SOCIAL MEDIA MOURNING

Social media mourning is defined here as the use of social media to mourn in a public way. Moore et al. (2019) undertook a study to explore how we use social networking sites to mourn. They examined one-way communication, two-way communication and immortality communication. The authors present a model of how mourners used social networking sites at the start of the bereavement process. The reasons for using social networking sites were to share information of the death and funeral, to mourn the loved one with others, to discuss broader issues of death with a wider community and to commemorate and reconnect with the dead. This study reflects both the findings of earlier work in this area and provides a useful model on which future research could be built, as presented in Figure 2.2. However, there is also a new phenomenon, which I term Mass Social Media Mourning, which is defined here as the idea that we are urged to mourn something that is not our grief through social media, such as the 2017 Manchester Arena bombing, or to mourn our personal loss through social media in a highly public way.

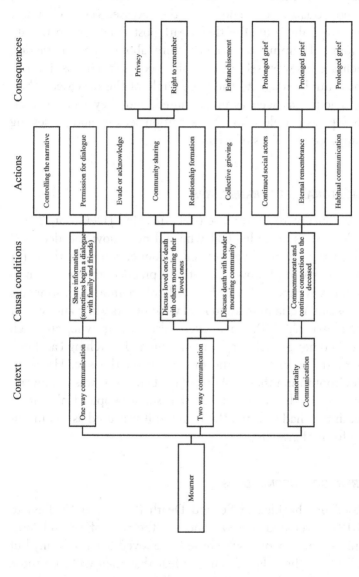

Figure 2.2 Social media mourning model (Moore et al., 2019).

BANDWAGON MOURNING

Bandwagon mourners are described by Rosetto et al. (2015) as individuals who did not know the deceased very well whilst they were alive but after their death posted a disproportionate amount of commentaries and pictures about them. In practice, their actions were seen as offensive because their position was not central enough to the close circle of the deceased. Their behaviour was seen as unwarranted, and they were invariably seen as people who were attention-seeking and possessing inappropriate levels of grief.

EMOTIONAL RUBBERNECKERS

The concept of emotional rubbernecking (DeGroot, 2014) is defined as an individual who did not know the deceased whilst they were alive, but felt a connection with them (or their survivors) following death. In practice, they are seen as 'online voyeurs who visit the Facebook memorials of strangers or distant acquaintances to read what others write and to post their own' (p. 79). There were also lurkers who, although they did not participate, were present and watching Facebook memorial groups and the discussion on the site. However, DeGroot found that rubbernecking behaviour was not always negative in that it was a way that some people dealt with a death that had affected them and so it was used as a communal form of grieving.

FEAR OF SECOND LOSS

Based on the idea of Second Death (Stokes, 2015; Bassett, 2018) developed a new concept: 'the fear of second loss'. This is where people who have lost a loved one physically but still retain their digital remains fear that they will lose those remains as well, so that they will have no enduring digital legacy. Bassett found that second loss was experienced negatively by the bereaved, and she explained:

> When I discussed with each of my participants how they would feel if the digital memories they had inherited were permanently deleted, their replies 'I would be devastated' and 'It would start my grief all over again' were implicit in all but one of my interviews. Even participants who did not visit Facebook pages or other accidental platforms commented that they would not want them switched off permanently, as they take comfort in the knowledge, they can switch them back on if they wanted to. One woman told me she was glad her mother's Facebook page was offline, but it still exists.
>
> Bassett (2018)

The idea of second loss (or digital erasure as Bassett also calls this experience) has become recognized as an increasingly important concern in the digital age, as important as the concept of the second death.

What is evident across the research and literature is that there remain relatively few norms for dealing with death in a digital age. The result is that spaces for mourning have expanded and become more complex, so that often norms are developed within the social media spaces and participants learn about mourning norms by being in such spaces. Yet it is evident in the work of Moore et al. (2019) that more people are turning to social media to deal with loss and yet it is unclear the kind of impact this is having on individuals, families and society as a whole.

CONCLUSION

What has become apparent is that the impact of these concepts, practices and decisions is having an (often detrimental) impact on the bereaved, with unintended consequences. The media portrayal of death in a digital age does point to the complexities of the relationships between death and the digital but also seemingly simplifies it. What is acceptable about how death is managed in public digital spaces is affected by social media norms as well as the death tech industry (Chapter 4). What is unclear is how the ethical challenges should be managed, and this is discussed next in Chapter 3.

3

ETHICAL MEMORIALIZATION

INTRODUCTION

This chapter begins by exploring what is meant by memorialization in a digital age and then moves to examine some of the ethical conundrums in this area. What it means to memorialize in ethical ways is explored, and the new area of the ethics relating to the creation of robots and digital immortals is examined. The later section of this chapter examines new rituals and practices such as hypermourning and the rise of death goods. Although this chapter considers a number of ethical concerns related to the use of death and dying, it is clear that this remains an emerging area of concerns.

MEMORIALIZATION

Memorialization in the digital age is becoming more common, commercialized and mostly sophisticated due to the increase in digital artefacts, death tech companies and diverse and accessible apps and social media being available. We are thus 'becoming better and better at leaving our survivors less to miss' (Buben, 2015: 16). Questions about ethical memorialization relate to whether digital legacies affect the way people feel about dying and the ways in which they choose to face or ignore death. For example, it is not clear whether the creation of digital immortals would mean that the deceased's funeral would be less meaningful or their memorial site was significant. Furthermore, it is still uncertain as to whether digital immortals affect or will change bereavement practices, resulting in a different kind of continuing bond, as will be discussed later in Chapter 6.

A useful way of considering the impact of digital immortals is suggested by Buben (2015). Buben refers to Interactive Personality Constructs (IPCs) by which he means the capturing of someone's appearance, mannerisms, voice and memories, as well as their view of different topics. These are then synthesized through recording and motion-capture techniques. What Buben is referring to is still in the development stages through companies such as Aura – as will be discussed in Chapter 4. Aura https://www.aura.page/ is a new site, created by Paul Jameson after he was diagnosed with motor neuron disease in 2017. Paul recorded his voice font before he became unable to speak and, in the process of dealing with this illness, he began to work with family and colleagues to develop a site that would be useful for those facing death. Such developments are more likely to be referred to in 2021 as digital immortals than IPCs. However, Buben challenges us to consider when we are creating an IPC (or a post-death avatar) whether the purpose is for recollection or replacement, which I define, based on his ideas as

- *Recollection.* an awareness of the loss of the person and what has disappeared following their death, and the preservation of memories of the loved one.
- *Replacement.* the creation of a post-death avatar to replace the dead loved one.

The issues of replacement bring to the fore questions about whether creating a replacement results in people becoming less concerned about the death and loss of a loved one. Replacement would seem to be about filling a void or particular role and thus using the dead as a resource for the living. It might be the case that replacement results in distraction from loss and interrupts the process of grieving, since the focus on creating a replacement is to ensure that the 'dead stay around'. However, whatever is created, in whatever form, brings with it issues about the ethics associated with different kinds of memorialization.

ETHICAL CONUNDRUMS

Much of the debate that occurs in the public sphere about digital memorialization in society focuses on the legal concerns and the terms and conditions imposed by different platforms – as discussed in Chapter 4. However, the ethical concerns stretch beyond the legal concerns since digital memorialization relates to the social good and thus introduces questions about what counts as the social good and who decides? Can or should everyone have the right to a post-death avatar? What will occur if such avatars become sentient? Are there different levels of digital memorialization that require different levels of ethical stances? Underpinning all of these questions is the need to delineate the values that inform the development, creation and management of digital memorialization, and the issue of values is central to this.

Kant (1998) distinguishes between conditional values and unconditional values. A conditional value is something valuable in some circumstances, whereas an unconditional value is valuable in all. According to Kant, the value of, for example, intelligence is conditional because we can imagine circumstances in which it would be bad for someone to possess it, such as when it would be used for evil ends. By means of this line of argument, Kant argues that 'the good will' is the only unconditional good, good in all circumstances. The good will is roughly a disposition to make morally commendable choices or to do the right thing.

The challenge then in terms of values is how artificial intelligence and digital immortals are likely to be shaped if there is no early intervention in the process of debate and instead commercial and corporate values and interests have a free rein. One insight into what might develop comes from a recent book by Zuboff (2019). In her book *The Age of Surveillance Capitalism: The Fight for a Human Future at the New Frontier of Power*, she argues that we have already entered a new and unprecedented era, that of Surveillance Capitalism, in which the dominance of the main technology companies, notably Google, Facebook, Apple and Amazon, has adapted capitalism to suit their own ends and over which the rest of us appear to have little or no control. In order to analyse this, she develops her own conceptuality. This form of capitalism is a new logic of accumulation based upon the realization that the apparently useless extra data that are now available through the mechanisms by which the digital can track both our movements, desires and behaviours, and produces a behavioural surplus which is then turned into prediction products. The technology companies extract these data without our consent or consultation, so we become the raw material and not even the product of this process. This means companies can reduce the levels of uncertainty about our future preferences, be those to do with consumption or politics and thus shape our behaviour towards guaranteed outcomes. Even though we may be aware of this, most of us seem content to trade off our privacy and the intrusion of such targeting for the supposed benefits of convenience and ease of communication. If this is then pursued into the field of AI and digital immortals, there are some potentially disturbing implications about the power of the few to determine the values incorporated into these new technologies. In some ways, this could be said to be happening in the early 21st century already.

ETHICS, ROBOTS AND DIGITAL IMMORTALS

What is clear from the review of the ethical conundrums is that there are two major issues: the first is that of agency and the second is that of how to engage and intervene in the developments that are yet to take place and how to influence or shape the values that will determine these. It is a matter of contention as to whether or not the current developments, which are often categorized as artificial intelligence, are in fact examples of machine learning where the outputs are no more than a result of the faster processing of the inputs, based on algorithms which can handle large amounts of data more rapidly than the human brain. This could perhaps be said to be the case when using machine learning to detect suicide risk on Facebook, as will be discussed later in this chapter. Yet there has been increasing realization that there needs to be a delineation between different types of ethics; robotics ethics, machine morality and intimacy ethics are all new areas that are being examined and have an impact on the relationship between artificial intelligence, death and dying.

ROBOTICS ETHICS

Malle (2016) argues that robot ethics needs to examine ethical questions about the relationship between humans and robots. He suggests that two issues need to be explored, both of which apply to virtual humans:

- Ethical questions about how humans should design, deploy and treat robots
- Questions about what moral capacities a robot should have.

Robot ethics features such topics as ethical design and implementation, as well as the considerations of robot rights. As mentioned in Chapter 1, Hern (2017) reported that

The European Parliament has urged the drafting of a set of regulations to govern the use and creation of robots and artificial intelligence. The report also takes a special interest in the future of autonomous vehicles, such as self-driving cars, but as yet there seems relatively little detail about how this might be implemented or developed, or indeed what the relationship between artificial intelligence and virtual humans is. However, in Autumn 2017 Sophia, a humanoid robot gave a speech at the United Nations, to prompt the recognition that there needs to be more debate, as well as legislation, in this area. As yet there has been no debate about the death of robots and indeed if this needs to be considered, not has there been any discussion about the use of robots for the care of the dying, in for example hospice settings. An issue that is of concern is that of intimacy ethics, particularly if robots are used to care for the dying.

MACHINE MORALITY AND INTIMACY ETHICS

Machine morality explores issues about what moral capacities a robot or virtual human should have and how these might be implemented. It also includes issues such as moral agency justification for lethal military robots and the use of mathematical proofs for moral reasoning (Malle, 2016). There are a range of debates on whether robots and virtual humans can have both emotions and empathy. For example, Prinz (2011) suggests that empathy is not needed for moral judgment whereas moral judgment does require emotion. However, Docherty (2016) argues that robots and robot weapons lack both emotions and empathy, and therefore cannot understand the value of human life, although should a robot (or virtual human) be judged to show emotions or empathy then this may no longer hold.

Using robots for caring and supporting humans offers people opportunities to connect with something emotionally and feel supported, even loved, without the need to reciprocate.

It is likely that such intimacy will develop in the near future as there is customer demand for this, particularly in countries such as Japan. For example, Kolstad et al. (2020) examined the process of integrating assistive robots into Japanese nursing care in 2019. The study sought to evaluate the use of robots from the perspective of and response from elderly people and nursing staff. The results pointed out that they were valued in terms of user satisfaction as well as having therapeutic and entertainment value. Yet the authors note that as yet it was felt that robot use was underutilized.

However, there are still considerable ethical, legal and social issues that need to be addressed in terms of robots. Some authors find relationships with virtual humans to be uncanny (Turkle, 2010), and for many people, marrying robots and substituting loved ones seems a step too far. Although this kind of inter-relationship is becoming more common (Levy, 2008), it introduces challenging questions about what it means to be human. Malle argues that:

> any robot that collaborates with, supports, or cares for humans—in short, a social robot—poses serious ethical challenges to the human design and deployment of such robots, and one of the most important challenges is to create a level of moral competence in these robots that is adequate to the application at hand.
>
> Malle (2016: 244)

Borenstein and Arkin (2016) argue that the main issues that need to be considered are affective attachment, responsiveness and the extent and duration of the proximity between the human and the robot. For example, Michel (2013) reported US military personnel forming attachments with bomb disposal robots. Emotional connection has also been found to be one of the strongest determinants of a user's experience, triggering unconscious responses to a system, environment or interface. Thus, an ethical concern is the extent to which a robot or virtual human affects a human's autonomy; for example, whether those people who have trouble forming human–human relationships will develop an over-dependent relationship with a virtual human or robot which reduces their ability to act as an autonomous human being. Furthermore, issues need to be considered about what happens if the robot is removed or malfunctions, and the person relying on it experiences loss and grief as a result of this.

DESIGN ETHICS

Digital immortals are designed using human decision criteria, and therefore, ethical behaviour needs to be 'designed-in' to them. Riek and Howard (2014) suggest that design considerations should include

- Reasonable transparency in the programming of the systems
- Predictability in their behaviour
- Trustworthy system design principles across hardware and software design
- Opt-out mechanisms (kill switches).

It is important to consider what occurs if autonomous combat robots or AI is deployed by the military and they mistakenly attack incorrect targets or fail to distinguish correct targets. Furthermore, in the context of the range of virtual humans that have been developed already, particularly those being designed for use pre- and post-death, designing appropriate and effective ethical standards remains complex and far reaching. As illustrated in Table 3.1, the complexity around design ethics in terms of creating a digital immoral raises a number of conundrums, which will be discussed further in Chapter 7 'Digital Afterlife Creation and Artificial Intelligence'.

Table 3.1 Ethics and Digital Immortals

Type of Avatar	Utilitarian Ethics	Deontological Ethics	Virtue Ethics	Situational Ethics	Discourse Ethics
Simple chatbots	A software programme that attempts to mimic human conversation when communicating with another (usually human) user. This type of chatbot can be created as an app which gives the illusion of talking to the deceased but is limited in its responses	If this benefits many people, then it is acceptable to use them	As long as its actions are innocuous, moral and of benefit this could be used.	The person programming this must a virtuous person	If this benefits people in a given context, then it is acceptable to use them	It is unlikely that a chatbot will be able to create discourse

(Continued)

Table 3.1 Ethics and Digital Immortals (*Continued*)

	Type of Avatar	Utilitarian Ethics	Deontological Ethics	Virtue Ethics	Situational Ethics	Discourse Ethics
Conversational agents	This is text-chat driven but can have associated imagery. It might be that more personality of the deceased may be shown in terms of conversational style	This may benefit many people, but it will be dependent on what is being provided, and the consequences of that provision	This may be of benefit as an information giving agent, but not if the conversation involves anything moral	It is unlikely that the agent can make virtuous conversation on sensitive tops and this could be a risk	If the context is appropriate, this can be used	This may be able to create discourse, but it is unlikely it would be able to deal with ethical issues

(*Continued*)

Table 3.1 Ethics and Digital Immortals (*Continued*)

Type of Avatar	Utilitarian Ethics	Deontological Ethics	Virtue Ethics	Situational Ethics	Discourse Ethics
Autonomous agent A software programme which operates autonomously according to a particular set of rules. Sometimes used synonymously with chatbots but in terms of creation of something post-death this might not operate as those left behind expect	Too much autonomy could be dangerous as it is difficult to predict the consequences of an agent	An autonomous agent would be too dangerous as it does not have a moral code or sense of duty	Virtues are affected by education class and context, and therefore, it would be difficult to devise a virtuous agent	Since an autonomous agent is unlikely to be to understand context, this may pose a risk	This may be able to create discourse, but ethical issues discussed could be risky
Pedagogical agent A virtual human used for educational purposes. The function of pedagogical agents is to aid learners during the learning process. These agents can support those left behind providing easier access to information	It is not clear if using an agent for teaching will have the right consequences, i.e. effective learning for most people	Using this would be acceptable if the agent was programmed to follow actions clearly	Teachers differ in the virtues they display; therefore, different types of virtuous agent would be needed.	This may work more effectively in some teaching contexts but not others	This could be used to help students understand the difficulties of discourse ethics and agents

NEW RITUALS AND PRACTICES

Although many death rituals in the 21st-century mirror traditional ones, such as funerals, burials, gravestones and remembrances artefacts, the digital has resulted in the creation of broader mourning spaces and places, as well as pre-death-related practices. Yet it remains unclear if these new rituals help engagement with the recognition and acceptance of death, or just result in death becoming another social media norm – as will be discussed in more depth in Chapter 7. This section provides an overview of just a few of the new rituals and practices.

DEATHTAINMENT

This is the mediatization of death announcement produced for popular entertainment. This activity is seen as part of the new forms of death cults, such as grief policing, media mourning and bandwagon mourning which are connected with an increasing interest in the portrayal of death in media spaces.

ROADSIDE MEMORIALS

Roadside memorials whilst not directly linked to artificial intelligence do bring a focus on the dead into everyday focus. An early example of this is the constant flower memorials left for the UK popstar Marc Bolan, lead singer of TREX. Bolan died in 1977 in a car crash when he was 29, and from the day of the accident, the site became a place of pilgrimage to Bolan fans and this was reported in various newspapers from 1978 onwards. A permanent memorial was erected on the site of the crash in 1997, some 20 years later.

Shrines of flowers, toys and messages present an idealized form of the life of the (often young) deceased. This mirrors media mourning practices whereby the dead are presented as angels with a constructed, idealized identity of the deceased.

For example, Walter et al. (2012) argue that the online dead are always accessible and often spoken about as angels. There is a sense then from Walter et al.'s perspective that angels have some kind of digital embodiment:

> Angels are messengers, travelling from heaven to earth and back, and cyberspace is an unseen medium for the transfer of messages through unseen realms, so there may well be a resonance between how some people imagine online messaging and how they imagine angels.
>
> Walter et al. (2012: 293)

COMMUNAL BONDS

Kasket (2012) suggests that an extension of the continuing bonds theory (Klass et al., 1996) should be that of communal bonds. In her study, she found that participants found that visiting Facebook and sharing grief was more helpful for many people than visiting a graveside or other form of memorial. Communal bonds are the continual posting on the person's wall, mostly to the dead person but to the associated community of mourners. Whilst this is now common practice, it is unclear if this is helpful in the grieving process, or whether it results in those left behind being stuck in a cycle of communal grief sharing.

HYPERMOURNING

Hypermourning is defined here (following Giaxoglou, 2020) as mourning through multiple media sources and also includes new forms of mourning often perceived to be overreactions to public deaths and public death events, such as celebrity mourning and global death. Giaxoglou (2020) suggests there are four types of hypermourning practices which include the

1. Type of loss which affects the way grief is shared
2. Intended purposes of memorialization
3. Duration of the mourning activity
4. Degree and types of activity on the site on which the memorial is hosted.

For example, after the death of David Bowie in 2016, the music and fashion industries both shared their grief on social media using images such as the thunderbolt, the signature sign of Bowie. A more recent example was the 2020 Covd19 pandemic, when social media became not only commentators but also the mediators of management of the crisis in the later stages of the pandemic, whilst governments (particularly the UK) were misrepresenting death figures and cultivating a culture of fear, and President Trump, the then president of the USA, flouted global guidelines in public.

TELLERSHIP

Tellership is either where those who have lost loved ones use their social media profiles to share their personal story of loss or where someone who is dying broadcasts their story. An important part of tellership is the role of the co-tellers who respond to the broadcasts and later offer tributes, thus creating a memorial, whether they knew them or not (Giaxoglou, 2020). An example is of Scott Simon, the National Public Radio reporter who live-tweeted his mother's death during her last days and hours. Cann (2014) suggests that Simon's use of Twitter marked three cultural shifts in the use of social media, in that it sanctioned the use of social media for documenting difficult events; social media was used to verify the importance of the event, and it provided updates in real time that made death a spectacle.

VIRTUAL VENERATION

This is the process of memorializing people through avatars in online games and 3D virtual worlds. An example of this is ancestor veneration avatars (Bainbridge, 2017), which are used as a medium for memorialising the dead and exploiting their wisdom by experiencing a virtual world as they might have done so. In practice, Bainbridge created a number of ancestor veneration avatars that were based on historical figures. These included three deceased religious innovators in three historically grounded virtual worlds which were Dark Age of Camelot based on 6th-century North Western Europe; The Secret World based on contemporary but historically based New England, Egypt and Transylvania; and A Tale in the Desert which simulates ancient Egypt. Within these worlds, Bainbridge employed different avatars to explore different historical events and practices. The historical figures were used in these role-playing games to enable the players to gain new perspectives about the meaning of the world, of society, of ethics and of the mortal self. The idea of such creations, Bainbridge suggests, begins to help us to see what digital immortality may look like and such work can help us consider the value of digital immortals, as will be discussed further in Chapter 7.

CONSUMER DEATH GOODS

Death goods are artefacts such as coffins, urns and plaques that are sold by funeral companies. In the 2000s, all of these can be bought on Amazon and in the USA from superstores such as Walmart. These are traditional goods, but it is also possible to buy more unusual goods such as bullets in which to place someone's ashes. Cann (2018) points out that consumer choices are not just based on cost but on beliefs about the afterlife. This would include issues such as what might help the deceased to make the transition to the afterlife and the value, or not of, embalming, burial or cremation. Recent innovations in death goods include designer coffins – that begin to look more like art installations and are available at Crazy coffins in the UK (https://www.crazycoffins.co.uk/index.html); ashes put into bullets, so they can be fired from your favourite weapon (Shooting your loved one's ashes https://www.inthelighturns.com/). It is also possible to create vinyl records.

And Vinyly https://www.andvinyly.com/ is a service, whereby using a teaspoon of someone's ashes, you can create a playable vinyl record. The companies tag line is that you can 'Live on from beyond the groove'. The cost of the record ranges between £1000 and £3000 depending on the specification and the quantity. Alternatively, EverWith (https://www.everwith.co.uk/) is a company that makes hand-crafted memorial jewellery including rings, pendants, earrings and bracelets. The cremation ashes are set in a choice of resin colours mounted on the jewellery. The company state that no ashes are discarded, and all unused ashes are returned to people. Whilst many of the artefacts are designed to be worn or kept, it is also possible to have a 'Space burial'. Instead of being shot from a gun, the ashes of the deceased are launched into space. This service is provided by the company Celestis. The company's official homepage states that the ritual consists of 'launching a symbolic portion of cremated remains into near-space, Earth orbit, to the lunar surface or even beyond' (Celestis, n.d.). It seems quite an odd choice since the living will watch it disappear, but the dead will have no knowledge of his experience.

GRAVE GOODS

Traditionally, grave goods were the items buried along with the body. These included personal possessions but also artefacts or food and drink designed to ease the deceased's journey into the afterlife, and provide them with what was needed in the after-life or in some cases they were offerings to the gods. Perhaps the most well-known grave goods are those found in Egyptian tombs which included not only gold and silver objects but also board games, chairs and clothing. Most grave goods recovered by archaeologists consist of inorganic objects such as pottery and stone and metal tools. The material objects discovered in Israel-ite tombs show they provided their dead with food and drink.

Today, grave goods are still buried with the dead and hold different significance depending on the religion. For example, The Bantu-speaking people of southwestern Zimbabwe (Nde-bele) kill an animal after burial in order to provide food for the journey ahead. In China, many people believe in leaving arte-facts such as paper fridges, paper money or phones at the grave-side for ancestors to use in the afterlife. The use of grave goods within funeral practice is linked to the ways in which different religions perceive the afterlife, as will be discussed in Chapter 5.

ARTIFICIAL INTELLIGENCE AND RISK

There is an increasing use of artificial intelligence to reduce various forms of risk. The first example provided here is the use of virtual life coaches in military forces in the UK. The second example is the implementation of machine learning for suicide prevention by Facebook.

A Virtual Life Coach (VLC) is a chatbot accessed by an individual through the web or their mobile phone, which can help with day-to-day personal, employment and career issues, maintaining motivation and supporting retention. The value of chatbots has been explored further in welfare and per-sonal support contexts (Kocaballi et al., 2019) as well as in alleviating anxiety and depression (Fitzpatrick et al., 2017). Mason-Robbie (2021) presents a study in which users were able to interact with a VLC in order to gain on-demand, specific, and personalized information. A mixed methods case study evaluation portrayed the views and experiences of users. Whilst many users found the VLC useful, overall the findings indicated that their use of the VLC did not provide sufficient reward in and of itself to motivate continued use. This echoes research identifying the importance of enjoyment and the presence of others in predicting attitudes towards using a social networking site for communicating with others (Jaafar et al., 2014) and also raises ethical conundrums about the extent to which bots and apps can really be used effectively to support mental health well-being and reduce personal risk. Facebook, however, developed machine learning tools in order to try to reduce suicide when it was identified on their site.

Due to the increase in suicide worldwide, Facebook undertook work to develop tools and resources is to help suicide prevention. In 2015, 78% of suicides accounted for 1.4% of all deaths worldwide and is deemed to be the leading cause of death among young people aged between 15 and 44. There has been an increasing interest in the use of the digital to support suicide prevention, exemplified by Siri, Alexa and Google Assistant, who have all enhanced their services to support suicide prevention. Whilst this software only uses keyword matching, it is a start. Other apps provide support such as Woebothealth, an app that is designed to help decrease anxiety and depression (https://woebothealth.com/) and SAM an anxiety management app (http://sam-app.org.uk/).

Facebook uses machine learning to detect the possible intent of suicide (Gomes de Andrade et al., 2018). The features they focus on are the content of the posts, the time of day and reactions to the posts; these classify the range of likelihood of suicidal intent. Gomes de Andrade et al. possess expertise in the area of suicide prevention and considered ethical concerns such as

- Whether Facebook should be developing and deploying prevention tools

- Balancing the issue of privacy and efficacy, they argue:
  When building suicide prevention tools, one of the balances we need to attain is between efficacy and privacy. These interests may be at odds with each other, as going too far in efficacy—detecting suicidal ideation at all costs, with no regards to limits or boundaries—, could compromise or undermine privacy, i.e., the control over your own information and how it is used. The question we were faced with was the following: How can we deploy a suicide prevention system that is effective, and that protects people's privacy, i.e., that is not intrusive and respectful of people's privacy expectations?

  Gomes de Andrade et al. (2018: 679)
- The use of machine learning intervention versus human intervention
- The choice of using machine learning thresholds to decide on the level of intervention.

The Facebook intervention offers an interesting and useful illustration of how artificial intelligence can be used for suicide prevention, but in practice, artificial intelligence intervention does not deal well with the ethical complexities involved. However, using artificial intelligence to deal with such a complex human problem as suicide prevention may be perceived to helpful to a degree but in fact it is rather an unsophisticated solution.

CONCLUSION

It is evident that memorialization is not unproblematic and that it continues to be an area of growth and innovation, but also a way that provoked diverse emotions and reactions. It is clear that digital memorialization in particular raises concerns for many people in terms of what happens to the digital legacies of the dead in terms of the response to, and responsibility for, the digital legacy. At the same time is remains uncommon for people to consider ethical questions about digital memorialization and there are also relatively few people who plan for the creation or ongoing persistence of their loved ones, as will be discussed next in Chapter 4.

4

DIGITAL LEGACY
MANAGEMENT

INTRODUCTION

This chapter begins by exploring issues of surveillance in order
to set the area of digital legacy management in context. It then
considers understandings of ownership in a time when social
media sites own, control and manage much of what is posted.
It then presents different forms of digital legacy and explores
the challenges of managing these. The second section of this
chapter explores the areas of ownership, security and privacy.
The final part of the chapter offers an overview of the death
tech industry and discusses the implications of this wide-
ranging and often covert industry on people's lives.

SURVEILLANCE AND TETHERED INTEGRITY

Surveillance is defined here as the monitoring of activities and
behaviour in order to influence, manipulate and manage people's lives. In the context of artificial intelligence, such monitoring occurs all the time in digital spaces, yet it often is seen
as more sinister and secretive than other kinds of surveillance.
As a result of social networking sites, personal data can be
mined and cross-referenced, sold and reused, so that people

are being classified by others through sharing their own data. Surveillance is liquid, Lyon argues, because it no longer keeps its shape, it flows and is now mobile:

> In a convenient confluence with liquid fear, liquid surveillance joins forces with everything from emergency preparedness drills to neighbourhood watches. In this way it also helps to beget its alter egos. If everyone is responsible for surveillance duty, everyone is also responsible for seeing to it that they are not surveilled against their will. Evading surveillance is in this view a problem of individual biography, not of institutional responsibility.
>
> Lyon (2010: 332)

Yet part of the difficulty with surveillance is that it can occur easily through artificial intelligence since few people control their privacy settings. It is possible to reduce surveillance by using privacy settings, and also increase social privacy by using pseudonyms and false accounts, regularly deleting wall posts and photographs and untagging from other peoples' posts.

Tethered integrity captures the idea that many of those who are always on and are digitally tethered do in fact have a degree of integrity about their use of social networking sites. Whilst some studies indicate that youth have more integrity in this area than adults (Brandtzæg et al., 2010), there is also an increased recognition of the power of such sites to manipulate what is shared, what is bought and the ways in which people behave. Tethered integrity should include the following judgments:

- Informed choice about which social networking sites are used and which are not, as well as how they are used and the privacy that is not only espoused but implemented

- Recognition and realistic control over the personal information that is shared, in ways that illustrate an appreciation of the personal benefit gained over the privacy lost
- Understanding the cost of surveillance and making informed choices about what that means in practice and whether it can be managed realistically
- Being aware of phone tracking and tracking through apps such as Twitter and making decisions about how this might be managed (or not)
- Being careful not to leave Bluetooth whilst shopping or in outside locations since this increases the possibility for surveillance and provides others with your information and provides them with free opportunities to track you
- Be aware of data mining programmes such as
  - PRISM, a clandestine mass electronic surveillance data mining program launched in 2007. PRISM is a tool used by the US National Security Agency (NSA) to collect private electronic data belonging to users of major internet services such as Gmail, Facebook and Outlook. Whilst it appears to be used less in 2021 than in 2019, it is still active
  - XKeyscore. This is a system used by the US National Security Agency for searching and analysing the Internet data it collects worldwide every day; it was revealed in July 2013 in Australia. There are some reports that this is no longer used but it is unclear whether this is the case.
  - Tempora, a clandestine security electronic surveillance program established in 2011 and operated by the British Government Communications Headquarters (GCHQ). Tempora uses fibre-optic cables to gain access to large amounts of internet users' personal data. The UK Government neither confirms nor denies the continuing existence of Tempora.
  - Stuxnet is a computer worm, which targets supervisory control and data acquisition systems and is believed to be responsible for causing substantial damage to the nuclear

program of Iran. It is thought Iran's Siemens software was infiltrated by the USA and Israel to limit Iran's nuclear capability. From the advent of Stuxnet and implications of extending and building on the software in open source, major oil and gas companies build significant cyber security systems for production platforms to reduce cyber-attack, damage at a cost of several hundred million US dollars.

In the past, there have been suggestions that there are sites that will provide privacy, but this is unlikely. What it does do is to suggest ways in which privacy can be improved to a degree.

LEVELS OF DIGITAL INTEGRITY

The following section suggests ways in which it is possible to improve, although not ensure, increased personal security. Although some people are more concerned than others, just being aware of what is available is important, even if it is not adopted:

High: this level is one in which people may choose to use their own server, block all surveillance traffic and use encryption wherever possible. Some examples of the types of software to enable this are described below, based on guidance from Estep (2013):

- Using Tor, a free software package that prevents anyone from learning location and browsing habits. It is an effective tool against network surveillance and traffic analysis.
- Using a virtual private network (VPN) to remove your place on the web and distract people attempting to locate you, for example setting your location to South America.
- Encrypting files and email using software such as Pretty Good Privacy Essentially. This uses key cryptography, so that messages can only be decrypted through a personal key file and the sender's public key. You can even encrypt files

so that only a specific person can open them. This is probably rather complicated for many people but is useful for the more technically savvy who want to communicate securely.

- Employing StartPage.com rather than Google for searching. It advertises itself as 'the world's most private search engine', allowing anonymous searching via Google. It is one of the few search engines that does not collect or share any personal information; another example is DuckDuckgo.
- Using Pidder, rather than Facebook, as this is a private social network that uses encrypted communication and offers the ability to remain anonymous.
- Taking the battery out of your phone. Whilst this might seem excessive, the only way a phone cannot be used to track/record is if the battery is taken out; it is interesting that many recent smartphones have non-removable batteries.
- Being aware of the safety of sites such as Zoom (Zoom bombing is the practice of trolling meetings which are not properly protected such as importing pornographic pictures into a religious meeting)
- Ensuring you know what data websites sites are collecting about you such as Snapchat

Medium: medium levels are for those who use social networking sites but accept that in doing so that they are subject to surveillance and location tracking which is inevitable. The suggestions here are therefore largely based on ensuring personal physical safety at home and work, and protection from virus attack.

- Using a secure wireless connection, so that other users can neither use it nor introduce unwanted and possibly dangerous traffic via it.
- Employing an effective firewall – and keeping it turned on, as well as using spam and spyware. It is important to know what services and sites are trying to send and receive data over your connection.

- Delete your cookies regularly – cookies are invariably used to track and collect data about you and the sites you visit; a useful plug-in to deal with this is called DoNotTrackMe.
- Disconnect your webcam as this can be secretly activated without the indicator light being on, so you won't even know that you are being watched or recorded.

Low or no integrity: Despite much warning about these dangers, there are many people who leave both location tracking and wireless connection permanently on, and do not log out of internet sites. Whilst many will not come to any immediate harm, it does mean that data are collected, people and their behaviours are tracked and personal safety and privacy can be at risk. What is perhaps more at risk is identity theft. For example, software such as Zeus is a Trojan Horse used for malicious and criminal tasks, such as stealing banking and credit card information. Furthermore, Giles explained

> The key to successful malware lies in tricking users into unwittingly installing it. And now even dilettante hackers can spread their malware by paying more technically adept criminals to do it for them.
>
> Giles (2010)

Government surveillance and the monitoring of our shopping habits has been taking place for many years; it is the sophistication that has changed. Yet amidst all of this, people do still have choice about what they engage with and by using high digital integrity, and moving platforms and social networking sites, privacy of sorts can be maintained to a degree. The question is the extent to which people really are concerned.

TYPES OF DIGITAL LEGACY

Digital legacy encompasses all the digital property left behind by the deceased, and these include digital remains, digital assets and digital traces, as well as digital endurance.

DIGITAL REMAINS

The concept of digital remains is used to describe the remains of the dead on social media sites and digital spaces such as photographs, websites and memes. Stokes (2015) in coining this term to describe the data of the dead suggests that seeing them as remains is raising the status of the data to that of a corpse. Morse and Birnhack (2020) undertook a national survey of the Israeli population and found a broad range of perceptions and practices about access to digital remains. What interesting was that their findings indicated low awareness of the available tools to manage digital remains, as well as reluctance to use them. What they noted is that platforms motivated by their own commercial interests tend to make their own policies since there is little legislative or judicial guidance.

A further difficultly with digital remains is that they continue to grow and proliferate as the number of dead people on Facebook continues to grow. Social media sites have become as Bassett (2020: 78) points out 'accidental' digital memory platforms and this continual growth is likely to become increasingly problematic, despite the introduction of Facebook's legacy contact appointed to manage Facebook digital estates post-death. This is partly because of the increasing number of the dead on Facebook as well as the controversies about what should be done with the digital estate and who decides this.

DIGITAL ASSETS

Digital assets relate to more tangible digital property than digital remains and tend in the main to refer to music, photographs and other assets stored on computers and clouds. There has been diverse media coverage relating to digital assets, one, in particular, about whether the actor Bruce Willis can leave his music collection stored on his Apple devices to his children or whether instead the collection would revert to Apple on his death. Rycroft explains:

> Digital photographs which have not been printed off, exist in a strange legal space where rights and responsibilities are often poorly understood. Music Libraries held online have often been purchased in some way by the user but are certainly not 'owned' by the purchaser in the same way a vinyl record or CD collection would be. The purchaser of an online music library has in effect purchased a licence to download and listen to the music and does not have the same right to pass on the music to a third party that the owner of a record or CD would have.
>
> Rycroft (2020:130)

Digital assets, whilst complex to administrate, do seem to be more manageable than remains which tend to exist on social network sites that have more complex terms and conditions, compared with property stored on the deceased person's computer.

DIGITAL TRACES

Digital traces are the traces, or digital footprints left behind by interaction with digital media. These tend to be of two types: intentional digital traces – emails, texts and blog posts; and unintentional digital traces – records of website searches and logs of movements. Accidental residents of the digital after-life who leave unintentional traces are seen as internet ghosts or the 'restless dead' (Nansen et al., 2015). The somewhat eerie consequences and the impact on recipients are unclear, particularly in relation to ancestor veneration avatars, where people are immortalized as avatars in online role-playing games (Bainbridge, 2013). The traces may be intentional creations pre-death, or unintentional for the dead but intentional by those left behind.

DIGITAL ENDURANCE

Bassett (2020) argues that digital endurance is a term that cap-tures enduring digital memories and messages posthumously, and suggests that for many bereaved people, these digital data contain the essence of the dead. Whilst her term refers directly to describe people's experiences of creating and inheriting dig-ital memories and messages, it is also increasingly used in the context of creating post-death avatars so that the dead can be reanimated (Table 4.1).

A recent study examined issues of digital legacy and legacy conditions. Cook et al. (2019) undertook a study of 32 ($n=32$) Australians over the age of 65 and identi-fied critical issues in the transfer, ownership, management and mobility of digital objects under legacy conditions. The authors suggest digital legacy management is a burden and that there is a need for regulatory reform in the pro-cess of making the transition from digital objects to digital assets. Studies such as this indicate there is still much legal work to be undertaken in this area of digital legacy world-wide as well as in the areas of postmortem ownership and postmortem privacy.

Table 4.1 Types of Digital Legacy

Type of Digital Legacy	Definition	Related Work
Digital remains	The bits and pieces that reflect the users' digital personality and, at the same time, compose the memories for the friends and family of the deceased users.	Morse and Birnhack (2020)
Digital assets	Any electronic asset of personal or economic value.	Harbinja (2017a) Rycroft (2020)
Digital traces	Digital footprints left behind through digital media.	Burden and Savin-Baden (2019)
Digital endurance	The creation of a lasting digital legacy; being posthumously present through digital reanimation.	Bassett (2020)

POSTMORTEM OWNERSHIP AND POSTMORTEM PRIVACY

There is often tension between the rights of the user to privacy, and the interests of the family and friends who may wish to access the digital legacy of the deceased. However, there is also an array of different terms relating to this, which are summarized in Table 4.2.

Many people believe that leaving a list of passwords behind is the best way forward so executors can gain access to information and assets stored on them. It is important to note that the use of someone else's password is contrary to the Computer Misuse Act 1990 Section 1, which expressly prohibits using the known password of a third party. Thus, it is important that none of this information is contained within the will

Table 4.2 Postmortem Ownership and Postmortem Privacy

Term	Definition	Related Work
Postmortem privacy	The right of the deceased to control his personality rights and digital remains postmortem, broadly, or the right to privacy and data protection postmortem	Harbinja (2017b)
Postmortal privacy	This is the protection of informational body – the 'body' that keeps living postmortem through the deceased's personal data, social networks, memes and other digital assets.	Harbinja (2020)
Postmortem ownership	The ownership of assets – physical and digital, by inheritors post-death	Rycroft (2020)
Digital estate planning	Organizing digital assets to ensure that these are handed over correctly to your dependents or loved ones	Rycroft (2020) Sofka (2020)

since it becomes a public document. The executors should know it exists but not be provided with it, and doing so may be breaching the terms and conditions of social media sites. The Data Protection Act (2018) relates to living persons only and terms and conditions are complex. Rycroft offers a list of useful steps to ensure that your beneficiaries can access your digital assets:

- Back up everything that is held on digital devices. If you back up into a cloud-based system think about what would happen if that failed or if you died and your subscription ended because your bank account was frozen or closed.

- Print off really important photographs and save videos offline. Technology is changing all the time and the devices we have today may not be compatible with those we have tomorrow.
- Transfer digital music libraries onto a portable device. The portable device is a physical object which can then be gifted to a beneficiary.
- Be mindful that some intellectual property rights enjoyed in life such as trademarks, patents and domain names are usually subject to renewal upon the payment of certain fees, so that these assets should be actively maintained in order to be preserved. The same may apply with regard to platforms used to store digital images such as Cloud based lockers and apps.
- Complete and keep updated a 'Digital Directory' which is a list on PAPER of your digital assets. Clearly such a document will help them be found upon loss of mental capacity or death and in the meantime the process of making and updating it may also help identify issues to be addressed.
- Think about any written material created online and make a decision about what is to happen post death and who will be in charge of it and who will benefit from its value; or whether you wish it all to be destroyed.
- Appoint a Digital Social Media Executor if you want a different person to have responsibility for that aspect of your digital life. Similarly utilise and engage with any protocols that digital platforms you use have available for this purpose, for example the Facebook Legacy Contact.
- Make a Will with a suitable expert and experienced solicitor, so that you can include all of your wishes with regard to your digital assets in a way which is clear, unambiguous and legally binding. Note under UK Law a person has to be an adult (aged 18 or over) to make a Will.

(slightly adapted from Rycroft, 2020: 141)

DIGITAL ESTATE PLANNING

Digital estate planning is the process of organizing your digital assets effectively to ensure that these are handed over correctly to your beneficiaries. Initially, this involves creating an inventory of digital assets and considering what dependents may need on death as well as considering what should be bestowed to whom. Digital assets include logins for social media accounts, blogs, investments, images, videos, files, messages, software, credit card reward points, bank accounts, shares, email accounts, websites and cloud storage. It is important to remember that not all digital assets can be shared, such as professional assets. Once all digital assets have been identified, they need to be stored securely and the executor named, and the executor needs to know how to locate the assets. One useful option is Cloud Locker (https://www.cloudlocker.eu/en/index.html) which is a cloud-based facility that you own and control physically as well as digitally, with patent-pending sharing and media control features. Other option includes the AfterVault (https://aftervault.com/) and Safebeyond (https://www.safebeyond.com/).

THE DEATH-TECH INDUSTRY

The death-tech industry is the growth of technology connected with death and bereavement. Whilst this includes the possibility for design and organizing a funeral online, the most recent growth, discussed below, is a series of companies who provide a range of services for recording pre-death memories to promising the possibility of an almost sentient post-death avatar of the deceased. It is noticeable that with developments in digital afterlife creation, there is an increasing interest in the management of death online despite much of the current software being an embellishment of the true possibilities. For example, the use of virtual assistants, such as Siri, that provide voice and conversational interfaces, the growth of machine learning techniques to mine large data sets, and the rise in the level of autonomy being given to computer-controlled systems, all represent shifts in technology that enhance the creation of digital afterlife. This section offers a summary of the developments in the death-tech industry. Over the last few years, there have been a number of sites, some of which now seem to be in abeyance, and these are described below as they may be redeveloped. A useful site that offers an overview of a number death-tech services is The Digital Beyond http://www.thedigitalbeyond.com/online-services-list/ however not all the links work. Below is a summary of what, in 2021, appear to be the main companies.

PREVIOUS DEATH TECH SITES

These two sites were popular, but in 2021, there appears to be little being offered here:

ETER9 (HTTPS://WWW.ETER9.COM)

Eter9 is no longer public, and what is at the address is just a holding page. Eter9 described itself as 'a social network that relies on artificial intelligence as a central element' and that 'Even in your absence, the virtual beings will publish, comment and interact with you intelligently'.

ETERNIME (HTTP://ETERNI.ME)

In 2021, Eternime links to a 2015 post, but it was a site where the individual was expected to train their immortal prior to death through daily interactions. As of July 3, 2018, 40, 497 people were signed up for their waiting list, but as of April 2021, little appears to be happening on the site.

CURRENT DEATH TECH SITES

These sites range from basic sites that just provide streamed funeral services with memorial pages, through to a complete planning package with tutorials and social media support:

MYWISHES (HTTPS://WWW.MYWISHES.CO.UK/ABOUT)

This began as DeadSocial (http://deadsocial.org); the idea behind this was to change the way society thinks about and prepares for death online through the provision of digital legacy and digital end-of-life planning tutorials. This site offers a number of tutorials which include preparing for death on social media sites (Facebook, Twitter, Instagram) and ways of downloading your media and data from social networks. It also offers 'funeral-tech tutorials' which includes arranging your own funeral and suggestions such as 'What 'Game of Thrones' can teach us about funeral planning'. The end-of-life planning tutorial offers useful suggestions about making relevant passwords available and an offline legacy builder which includes creating a will and social media will. My Wishes has developed considerably in 2020 and now offers a free planning app, and it has been using social media to and television to gain support and interest.

LIFENAUT (HTTPS://WWW.LIFENAUT.COM)

Lifenaut enables people to create mindfiles by uploading pictures, videos and documents to a digital archive, but this is an explicit process. It also enables the user to create a photo-based avatar of the person that will speak for them, although there is the choice of only a single male and female voice which are both US English. Lifenaut is a product of the Terasem Movement Foundation (http://www.terasemmovementfoundation.com/), which describes its work on Lifenaut as being to investigate the Terasem Hypotheses which state that

1. A conscious analogue of a person may be created by combining sufficiently detailed data about the person (a 'mindfile') using future consciousness software ('mindware'), and
2. That such a conscious analogue can be downloaded into a biological or nanotechnological body to provide life experiences comparable to those of a typically birthed human.

In practice, Lifenaut offers a number of ways to build a 'mindfile'. These include

- Just talking to a few sample bots, although the conversations seem non-sensical and they appear to ignore what you say.
- Filling out some interview questionnaires, including some 'validated' personality profiles, including a 486-question personality survey measuring cautiousness, conscientiousness, cooperation, gregariousness and nurturance.
- Talking to your own avatar so it learns from what you say, although this appears to require an explicit 'correction' action.
- Manually adding favourite things and URLs, although your bot does not appear to learn them once added.

It is also claimed that it is possible to have your mindfiles beamed continually into space for later potential interception and recreation by alien intelligences. The grandiosity of some of the claims made here is not all empirically testable. Furthermore, the idea of creating a digital archive for future use raises questions about the impact of life stage at death, as the experiences of people at different stages of the life span will impact on the legacy left behind, such that an afterlife may become 'stuck' at a particular stage without moving forward with those who are left behind, as discussed later in Chapter 6.

DADEN (HTTPS://WWW.DADEN.CO.UK/)

The work of Daden and the University of Worcester (Burden & Savin-Baden, 2019) in the UK aimed to create a virtual human, which is a digital representation of some, or all, of the looks, behaviours and interactions of a specific physical human. This prototype system contains relevant memories, knowledge, processes and personality traits of a specific real person and enables a user to interact with that virtual persona as though they were engaging with the real person. The virtual persona has the individual's subjective and possibly flawed memories, experiences and view of reality. The information provided by the individual is in a curated form and, as such, only data the individual chooses to share will be included in the virtual persona. Whilst the project has focused on the use of such persona within the sphere of corporate knowledge management, the mere existence of the virtual persona and virtual life coaches immediately raises issues around its digital afterlife. The virtual life coach project is described in more detail in a forthcoming book by Savin-Baden in a chapter by Mason-Robbie (2021).

RECORDMENOW APP (HTTPS://RECORDMENOW.ORG/)

This is a free app that enables people to create a video legacy. It works by using questions to prompt people. The website offers training workshops for organizations in the areas of leaving a loving legacy, living with dying, caring for carers at end of life and supporting children, when someone close is dying. The app is easy to use and the questions used prompt reflection in different life areas, so that is possible to build a story over time with short, easy to record, videos. It can be used on a pc as well a cell phone and also offers guidance on liturgy for different faiths. The terms and conditions do not appear to deal with issues of ownership of the digital legacy.

AURA (HTTPS://WWW.AURA.PAGE/)

This is a site created by Paul Jameson after he was diagnosed with motor neuron disease in 2017. Paul recorded his voice font before he was no longer able to speak and in the process of dealing with this illness, he began to work with family and colleagues to develop a site that would be useful for those facing death. The focus of this site is in assisting people in creating a legacy and preparing properly to discuss, manage and celebrate life and death. The site in late 2020 comprises a series of videos to guide people, as well as useful articles on everything from funerals to virtual humans. It is early in its development, but it is striking and well presented and seems to offer a realistic stance to issues of managing the process of moving towards death and issues of digital afterlife.

ELIXIR (HTTPS://WWW.ELIXIRFOREVER.COM/)

This US company argues that before the COVID 19, most people spent 7 hours a week online and that this has grown since then. What they point out is that post-death, social media sites may freeze accounts – such as Instagram. Facebook offers a legacy contact to manage the site or the option to memorialize it and Twitter accounts can be frozen if proof of death is shown. The strap line is 'Dedicated to using AI and neural network technology to empower your digital AI self in this lifetime'. The company suggests that we need to create an authentic digital copy to enable our family and friends to continue to connect with us. The solution they propose is for us to use social media to create our own AI being which has a 'digitally positive carbon negative foot print', but the website does not say how this will be achieved.

ANKHLABS (HTTPS://ANKHLABS.IO/BEANKH/)

This German company states that it brings together artificial intelligence, big data and blockchain technology to 'add immutability' to digital immortality, through an app entitled BeANKH.

The BeANKH app applies AI to social media such as face recognition, emails communication, bot and block chain technology to build your own look-a-like digital assistant 3D avatar which uses a digital copy of your voice. They suggest it is possible to preserve and share people's essential traits and personality long after their physical death. The use cases they cite vary from what would appear to be using a bot as a personal assistant to more innovative options. However, to date there are many other companies offering examples of personal assistant and virtual mentors, particularly in the mobile space where the interaction can seem particularly intimate and personal. Examples include Wysa (https://www.wysa.io/) and Woebot (https://woebot.io/) along with apps for behavioural interventions for at-risk drinkers and free physical activity coaching apps.

The BeANKH app enables you to undertake activities in day-to-day life such as

- The AI Gaming Bot lets your digital copy play boring parts of games for you, whilst you do other things.
- The Birthday Manager lets your digital copy remind you about birthdays, proposes compliments and presents.
- The Social Media Manager enables your digital copy like and comment for you on social media.
- The Automated Dating function enables your digital copy to make a pre-selection of dating candidates for you on dating portals such as Tinder.

- The Personal Assistant allows your digital copy to organize appointments and answer messages for you.
- Visual Gaming Avatar uses your digital copy appearance and voice as live avatar in games.

There are other options that may be financially risky and offer opportunities for accounts to be hacked, which include the following:

- You can rent your digital copy to other BeANKH users as a digital friend to gain income.
- The Shopping Manager enables your digital copy to inform you about latest shopping trends based on your personal preferences – however, Amazon and other shopping sites already do this.
- The Working Bot rents your digital copy to fulfil specific tasks and earn money.
- Fake Profile Detector helps you to detect fake profiles of you on social media channels and propose actions – which is a useful idea but it is not clear how this will be undertaken.

In terms of artificial intelligence, death and dying, there are other services which overlap with other death-tech sites, for example, you can arrange to

- Record messages that can then be sent on a certain date in the future or after personal death
- Transfer cryptocurrencies in your BeANKH Secure Wallet with a handover date post-death.

More innovative options available from ANKHLABS include the possibility of creating a Robot Controller that control humanoids or other type of robots with your digital copy and the ability to connect your digital copy, with augmented reality and virtual reality hardware such as Microsoft HoloLens – an untethered mixed reality device with apps and solutions that are designed to enhance collaboration. This company appears to be providing an extensive range of services, but currently much of it does seem to appear to be more of a personal assistant than any kind of digital afterlife creation. Furthermore, despite the options for creating post-death recording and money transfers there does not appear to be any support or link to bereavement services, as with other sites.

ITENAL.LIFE (HTTPS://ITERNAL.LIFE/)

This site focuses on using storytelling to create memories, very much like Recordmenow. The home page asks you to record your memories, but you need to sign up to do this. It then asks for personal details before you can progress further. The focus here is on helping families save their memories for generations to come, so it is really a site where you can record and save memories and probably little more than this.

DIGITAL IMMORTALITY NOW (HTTP://DIGITAL-IMMOR-TALITY-NOW.COM/)

This site's strap line is 'The instrument to reach immortality for everyone'. The site suggests that it is possible to provide cheap and affordable digital immortality for everyone. It seems to be a site where people upload self-recording and self-description to facilitate future reconstruction. The site provides a long article on digital immortality and the possibilities for the future, but does not really explain how this will be undertaken. Some of the steps suggested to create immortality include collecting your DNA, collecting existing data such as photos, documents and video, extracting personal data from social networks, running psychological tests, interviewing friends and creating art. The steps suggested seem little different from other sites; for example, they advocate a number of steps to achieve digital immortality creation – which in fact is really just the creation of a digital legacy. Other parts of the site seem to be presenting futuristic transhumanism, with articles to support this stance.

IN SUMMARY

When exploring the scope and type of these sites, it is noticeable that most of them only tend to be accessed by those consciously and deliberately preparing for death, beyond the common cultural practices of creating a will and, for some, planning or expressing wishes about a funeral. What is important when using any of this software is to read and understand the terms and conditions as these can be confusing and it is not always evident whether the copyright belongs to the company or the person who creates the content. Terms and conditions need to be realistic and understandable and deal with issues of ownership and privacy. As Rycroft (2020) argues, legal provision to date in this area is an area of concerns and one where many lawyers remain unsure of the way forward. It is also noticeable that the growth of sites and services offering chatbots continues to grow, but it is not yet clear which ones are likely to provide a genuine and feasible post-death bot or avatar or whether much of it is hopeful advertising. For example, Collins (2021) reported the possibility that the patent filed by Microsoft could enable people to be reincarnated people as a chatbot. The system would use social media, images and electronic messages to build a profile of a person. However, privacy issues are not discussed, nor is the ability to opt out of being created as a bot. Again, it is not clear how realistic this is or whether it is just a marketing ploy.

CONCLUSION

This chapter has explored issues of surveillance and perspectives on digital legacy, as well as presenting various sites which enable digital legacy creation and suggest the possibility for digital immortality. It is evident that platforms and businesses still control much of what is unloaded and even digital legacy sites do not have clear terms and conditions about what will occur if the sites are deleted or those with access to the data die. For those wanting to create a digital legacy, it is probably safer not to undertake this on a digital legacy site but collect information on a person computer and store it on a portable device that can be left with loved ones. What is also clear from sites such as digital immortality now is that there are still those with a utopian sense of what it is possible to achieve in the area using artificial intelligence. The use of artificial intelligence to create digital immortality and digital afterlife is not straight forward and also has religious implications, which will be discussed next in Chapter 5.

5

RELIGIOUS PERSPECTIVES

INTRODUCTION

This chapter begins by examining the meaning of death and exploring religious engagement with artificial intelligence. It then examines theologies concerning death and then presents perspectives on death and artificial intelligence in relation to six different belief systems, namely Christianity, Humanism, Sikhism, Buddhism, Hinduism and Islam. It is clear that although different religions are beginning to explore that relationship between their religion and artificial intelligence, few, if any, is examining it in relation to death and dying within specific religious contexts.

DEATH, RELIGION AND ARTIFICIAL INTELLIGENCE

It is currently unclear whether artificial intelligence undermines or enables creative religious engagement with death or not. There is often a public perception that artificial intelligence and religion cannot mix, but equally, there is a tendency to neglect the impact of religion on society. As illustrated in Chapter 4, the death tech industry provides 'solutions' to death and afterlife that are many and varied. It might be the case that artificial intelligence appears to soften the reality of death or alternatively helps to create the illusion of limitless human beings. The idea of losing the sense of our limits may result in something being lost in the religious and spiritual sense, with the result that we become immune to the possible impact and thus when someone dies, there is a greater shock about the impact of it on our lives. Many religions see artificial intelligence as something that cannot replace human beings, in terms of artificial intelligence representing or taking the place of a religious figure.

Herzfeld (2002) offers an interesting exploration of what it means for human beings to be created in God's image and approaches towards creating artificial intelligent beings. Her perspectives are summarized in Table 5.1.

Whilst Herzfeld (2002) offers some interesting views on the relationship between humanity being created in the image of God and artificial intelligence, a more useful is a more up to date perspective is that

> … widely available virtual humans could have a significant impact on a number of different aspects of society. The 'rise of the bots' may not even be restricted to low and mid-skills. Companies such as DoNotPay are already providing virtual humans to enable people to challenge parking fines (Gibbs, 2016), the UK's National Health Service is testing an AI chatbot developed by Babylon Health (https://www.propelics.com/healthcare-chatbots), and Woebot (https://woebot.io/) is a virtual counsellor employing cognitive behavioral techniques to help address negative thinking.
>
> Burden & Savin-Baden (2019: 252)

The types and range of artificial intelligence can also be seen in other practical outcomes as exemplified in the following areas:

Table 5.1 Artificial Intelligence and the Image of God

Type of Artificial Intelligence	Definition (These definitions have been based on Herzfeld's article, but in 2021, there are more complex definitions of artificial intelligence)	Artificial Intelligence and the Image of God
Symbolic artificial intelligence	Creating computer programmes that could 'understand' and manipulate symbols in order to reason, also called the cognitivist approach.	Human intelligence comprises reason and the management of unconscious and conscious knowledge; thus, an artificial intelligent being would need to be more than a symbol reader
Functional artificial intelligence	This is the use of artificial intelligence to undertake basic tasks	Whilst artificial intelligence is used for the completion of tasks, the creation of an artificial intelligent being created as an image of a human would be purely task orientated and thus not reflect the image of God
Relational artificial intelligence	This is what is generally now seen as machine learning, the process of teaching a computer system how to make accurate predictions when fed data	A relational artificial intelligent being needs to communicate by hearing, listening and being able to give and receive gladly.

PRAYER BOTS

Öhman et al. (2019) undertook a study that examined Islamic prayer apps. The purpose of such apps is to support and automate worship, but it is also used to support and encourage the process of asking for a wish to be fulfilled. However, in terms of artificial intelligence, the app is used to support post-death progress, as discussed later in this chapter:

> Arguably, one of the core functions of the automated prayer apps is tied to their explicit promise to continue posting even after the user's death. For instance, the slogan of Zad-Muslim.com reads "Register now so your account would tweet now and after you die." Similarly, Dur3a.org promises that "your account will tweet in your life and in your death."
>
> Öhman et al. (2019: 335)

Bots and apps are also used in other ways such as the Church of England's voice activation software feature for Alexa which can read daily prayers. Catholics also may use an app to participate in the Pope's prayers using the Click to pray app, and Jewish communities are also using artificial intelligence to automate activities in their home during the Sabbath, from timers to more complex technology (Woodruf et al., 2007).

GOD, HUMANS AND ARTIFICIAL INTELLIGENCE

Haeker (2019) argues that conversations about artificial intelligence have largely been conducted in the context of a secular framework. He suggests that it is a mistake to believe that technology could be an addition to the nature of God. However, whilst his stance is interesting, I suggest that is not perhaps what most of us believe; rather most people consider technology can be used to enhance humans through longevity and to transcend death rather than used to enhance the nature of God. The relationship between humans and artificially intelligent beings also introduces questions about whether they can have beliefs and have a soul or whether they will necessarily be atheists.

RELIGIOUS LANGUAGE AND ARTIFICIAL INTELLIGENCE

There have been a number of studies and explorations of the use of artificial intelligence in religious contexts, such as Muslim religious leaders' perspectives of artificial intelligence, discussed later in the chapter. An experiment undertaken by Reed (2019) used a plagiarism detection entitled EMMA to examine biblical text in order to establish authorship and found that length and style affected the ability to detect accurately. In a different study, Singler (2020) explored tweets that mention the phrase 'blessed by the algorithm' in order to examine popular concepts of artificial intelligence as divinity. The phrase is used by people to suggest that they have been fortunate in receiving content fed to them on social media platforms, whether in terms of affirmation or jobs offered or suggested. Singler found seven types of tweets about being blessed by the algorithm, and these included

1. User hope of being blessed by the algorithm
2. Response to recommendation for that day such as music and shopping
3. Being blessed by finding work through gig economy job – the term 'gig economy' refers to small tasks or jobs (the 'gigs') that individuals are contracted to carry out. These jobs are allocated digitally, invariably through algorithmic management methods (Tassinari & Maccarone, 2020).

4. Just saying or feeling blessed by the algorithm in a vague unconnected way
5. Using religious language by non-religion people to argue for being blessed
6. Negative responses such as being cynical about the current state of affairs or people's successes
7. References to science fiction characters, concepts and plotlines.

What is particularly interesting about both the idea of being blessed by the algorithm and the way in which tweets are used is that there is an assumption of blessing, beginning with an assumption that blessing through artificial intelligence technology is not only a possibility but a reality.

ARTIFICIAL INTELLIGENCE AND PLACES OF WORSHIP

Whilst there are various understandings of what counts as places of worship the discussion begins by examining churches. As far back as 2009, Estes took up the challenge to defend online churches:

> If we read carefully the criticisms levied against internet campuses, they boil down to some very common and tired themes: Internet campuses and online churches are not true churches because they don't look like and feel like churches are expected to look like and feel like (in the West, anyway). Arguments against virtual church follow the idea that if it doesn't look like church, feel like church, swim like church, or quack like church, it's not a church. This may be a useful test for ducks, but churches are far more complex animals.

Online churches today are seen as more acceptable than in 2009, especially since the advent of the COVID-9 pandemic.

The most 'fertile' virtual world for church used to be in the virtual world Second Life, where over 100 churches were developed, with some being more active than others. Second Life was a 3D virtual world, rather than a game, launched in 2003 by Linden Lab. Virtual worlds are defined as having five main characteristics which separate them from other forms of social networking or gaming, using computer technologies (Savin-Baden & Falconer, 2016). These are

- Persistent, since changes that are made in-world remain, and the world continues to develop and be active, whilst individuals are logged off the world.
- Synchronous, so that participants in-world are all present at the same time, regardless of their real-world location.
- Social, because users can interact with each other through various means of communication such as voice and text chat, and through experiences such as dance, making music, building and developing.
- Visually interactive, so that users interact with each other and the world through their avatars. It is important to recognize that those users need not be human; bots, non-player characters and avatars driven by artificial intelligence are commonly encountered in VWs.
- Visually rich, since they contain a wide range of visually detailed 3D environments, often enhanced by the ability to change the time of day or the weather, and to add sound and music.

Whilst some may wonder at the value of these kinds of churches, and some have argued vociferously against them (Hyatt, 2009), authors and researchers such as Campbell suggest that they support rather than replace face-to-face church. Furthermore, Hutchings studied five examples of online churches and suggests that between two-thirds and three-quarters of the members of each were attending a local church regularly (Hutchings, 2010). A recent example is the virtual reality church https://www.vrchurch.org/ which uses the AltSpace software. The focus is to explore and communicate God's love through virtual reality, augmented reality and next-generation technologies. There are also Muslim sites, such as Virtual Mosque https://www.virtualmosque.com/aboutus/ which provides guidance, videos and teaching. There are also virtual tours of mosques but few spaces in which virtual worship takes place. There are Hindu worship apps and temple tours but little in the way of virtual spaces for worship. There is live streaming of Buddhist services available https://www.buddhistchurchesofamerica.org/live-streaming-and-recorded-temple-services/ and it is possible to download a copy of the readings and chants to be used. However, more recent developments in artificial intelligence and religion relate to the Turing church.

TURING CHURCH

The Turing Church defines itself as a group of people who are at the intersection of science and religion, spirituality and technology, engineering and science fiction, mind and matter. They have a Facebook page and links with the transhumanist movement. The Turing Church argues that they create 'theism from deism', as Prisco explains

> I am persuaded that we will go to the stars and find Gods [extra-terrestrial intelligence], build Gods [AI], become Gods, and resurrect the dead from the past with advanced, space–time engineering and 'time magic'
>
> Prisco (2018)

The doctrine of the Turing church is based on the ideas and visions of Prisco who is one of the founder members of the church and also a transhumanist. There are two models for god: natural god, which seems to have similarities to the Christian Trinitarian God and a systems operator god, which controls us as information bits that live and move in a super-computer beyond space and time, operated by a god-like operator. What is interesting about this approach to artificial intelligence is the sense that this group of people believe that it will be possible to play with space, time, matter, energy and life and that we will be resurrected by very advanced science and technology. However, there is little indication of how this might happen.

There is little discussion about religious responses to the relationship between death and artificial intelligence and few if, any, discussions about the creation of pre- and post-death avatars. This area will be examined later in this chapter, but it is first important to examine the idea of theologies of death.

THEOLOGIES OF DEATH

Theologies of death encompass issues such as ideas of belief, afterlife, liturgy, heaven, hell ritual and disposal. Davies (2008) suggests that a starting point for exploring the theology of death is Schweitzer's question of 'whether death resides inside you ...' whether 'you have conquered it within and settled your account with it' (Schweitzer, 1907/1974: 67). Davies' theological stance towards death is that it should be seen in terms of a relationship between lifestyle and death style; the idea that a theology of death must also be a theology of life. For example, if death is seen as the absurd, as empty nothingness then life should reflect some of these attributes. In short, our life-style challenges our death style. It is clear that theologies of death are complex and wide ranging but can be grouped into two main areas: the problem of death and the theological understanding of the mystery of death.

The problem of death. This seems both natural and absurd both for atheists and for those of faith. Death is a puzzle, and as no one has experienced or really understands it, it is absurd. Camus depicts this particularly in *L'Etranger* (Camus, 1942a), which portrays the futility of a search for cohesive meaning in an incomprehensible universe without God. However, his perspective on the absurd is perhaps best captured in the *Le Mythe de Sisyphe* (Camus, 1942b), whereby Sisyphus pushes a rock up the mountain, watches it roll down and pushes it back up again in an endless cycle. Camus' point is that like Sisyphus, humans continue to question the meaning of life, but remain troubled by the answers continually falling away. However, even for those with a faith, the mystery of death remains problematic, but there is also an excitation of some kind of divine revelation as a solution to this problem

The theological understanding of the mystery of death. The wide body of literature on this topic remains controversial. What is clear is that there is little understanding of what happens to the soul after death. Some believe it is affected by prior choices made when the soul is in the state of union with the body, whilst others suggest there may be possibilities for growth and development post-death.

What is important in any kind of theology of death in the digital age is that it should assume that death is contextual and needs to be fluid and that it should not assume that death is manageable or explicable. However, it is clear that in most of the literature that explores theologies of death the focus is largely on hope, which necessarily seems to imply there is a straightforward answer to death, rather than the need to problematize it. This might account for the idea of hope in the creation of post-death avatars and the perceived value of digital legacy creation.

Furthermore, the meaning of death differs across religions and this therefore has an impact on how death and the afterlife are perceived in relation to artificial intelligence.

RELIGIOUS PERSPECTIVES ON ARTIFICIAL INTELLIGENCE

Although there are over 4,000 religions in the world, six religions' stances towards Artificial intelligence are presented here, along with views from people of faith. Each section provides a basic overview of the faith's doctrine and a stance towards artificial intelligence.

JUDAISM

In Judaism the belief is that life does not begin with birth, nor does it end with death. This is articulated in the book of Ecclesiastes 12 v 7, 'And the dust returns to the earth as it was, and the spirit returns to G-d, who gave it.' Central to Jewish faith is the belief in *techiat ha-meitim*, (resurrection of the dead) and that the soul will be restored to a rebuilt and revitalized body. For Jews the soul is the higher, more spiritual incarnation of the self, but they maintain a high respect for the body, since it is seen as the mechanism which enables all the soul's accomplishments during life.

Jews do believe in an afterlife but the formulation of this varies; there is a sense that the soul journeys, passing such things as *Dumah* an angel of the graveyard, and Satan as the angel of death on the way towards *Gan Eden* - heavenly respite, or paradise. Jewish eschatology combines the Resurrection with the Last Judgment. Resurrection is referred to in the book of Ezekiel, Chapter 37 as only being for Jews, but later resurrection underwent a change, and was made part of the Day of Judgment on the basis of Daniel 11v 2. The resurrection includes both the righteous who awake to everlasting life and the wicked who face shame and everlasting horror. Those who believe in God's judgement, believe the decision about whether they should be rewarded or punished is based on how well they have followed the mitzvot -the Jewish laws and commandments.

CHRISTIANITY

Whilst there are varying beliefs about what happens post-death, one straightforward argument has been presented by McDannell and Lang (2001) who suggest that either the entire person will be resurrected or the soul goes to heaven and the body is left on earth. Gooder (2011), however, suggests that there is a need to rethink the idea of the soul:

> … the Hebrew often translated as 'soul' (e.g. Ps 62.1 'For God alone my soul waits in silence') is often elsewhere translated as 'life' (e.g. Ps 59.3, 'Even now they lie in wait for my life'). The two are almost interchangeable in the Hebrew Bible and the words in italics translate the same Hebrew word, nepesh.

This suggests a separation of the soul from the mind and the body. Before a belief in resurrection emerged life after death in the Hebrew Bible was not about resurrection, but about the continuation of the family line, which was why the birth of a son was so important then. Life and death were highly relational events in traditional Israel, bound up in community and with a focus on 'biological immortality', the importance of transmitting our genes via our descendants. Recent studies, such as Cook (2007), make cross-cultural comparisons which explain the vital role of the dead in maintaining ties through lineage and tenure of and burial on ancestral land.

Whilst many Christians are concerned about the impact of artificial intelligence on faith, life and employment

(Schuurman, 2019), there are others who like Haeker (2019) reflects:

> to ask the question of artificial intelligence is at once to ask a recognisably religious question about the first beginning and final purpose of our souls in their relations to God, the stories of myth, of revelation, and of history which we choose to tell about the origin, nature, and purpose of minds and machines, can thus inform any possible expectation of the destiny of artificial and human intelligence.

The Bishop of Oxford Stephen Croft is a member of the House of Lords Select Committee on Artificial Intelligence, and his stance is that what should be central to develop is an ethical stance. He recognizes the value of artificial intelligence for good in terms of medicine, efficiency and transport, but also the dangers of inequality, effects on mental health and the manipulation of data. His views have been part of the report AI in the UK: ready, willing and able? (House of Lords, 2018). However, there are also concerns about what would happen where robots are able to make copies of themselves; McGrath asks:

> Would androids have the capacity to make backup copies not only of their data and memories, but the precise configuration of their neural networks, so that, in case of death, a new copy could be made that would continue from where the original left off? More importantly, would such a copy, restored from backed-up software, be the same person?
>
> McGrath (2011, n.p.)

McGrath continues this line of questioning by exploring the issues of afterlife and if it were possible to have copies of ourselves would they experience eternal life, which is certainly a challenging theological question, but not one that would trouble Humanists.

HUMANISM

Humanists have no belief in an afterlife, and so they focus on seeking happiness in this life. They rely on science for the answers to questions such as creation, and base their moral and ethical decision-making on reason, empathy and compassion for others. Humanists argue that human values make sense only in the context of human life and therefore existence after death is not part of the humanist value system. The current world is the focus of their ethical concerns and aspirations and therefore the values they hold are placed in the context of the here and now. However, the Sikh stance is on both doing good now and celebrating the future with God.

SIKHISM

Sikhs believe that upon death, one merges back into the universal nature. Sikhs do not believe in heaven or hell as places where the dead go. Heaven can be experienced by being in tune with God whilst still alive. The bodies of the deceased will later be cremated, but their souls will live on, Sikh tradition teaches. Sikh scriptures do not dwell on what happens after death. Instead, the faith focuses on earthly duties, such as honouring God, performing charity and promoting justice. Sikhs believe in karma or 'intentional action'. As one Sikh explained:

> I believe your soul joins the Almighty when you die. In practice in my religion there is the vague notion of a 'good place' where the Almighty welcomes the souls of those who have followed the principles of the religion, undertaken seva and an honest living whilst those who have not are condemned to the cycle of rebirth

Through good actions and by living a good life and keeping God in their minds, Sikhs hope to achieve good merit and avoid punishment. In Sikh theology, living morally prepares the soul to receive God's grace. For those fortunate enough to escape rebirth, the ultimate destination is a return to the divine soul from which all beings emanate. The tradition also teaches us that death is something worth celebrating, because the souls are going to be one with God. In terms of an artificially intelligent being, Sikhs believe that it would have no soul, and if there is no soul, there is no true consciousness, no real death, no reincarnation and no salvation.

BUDDHISM

Buddhism teaches that an individual is but a transient combination of the five aggregates (skandhas): matter, sensation, perception, predisposition and consciousness and so has no permanent soul. The human being is an assemblage of various elements, both physical and psychical, and none of these individual aspects of a whole person can be isolated as the essential self; nor can the sum of them all constitute the self. Since a human is composed of so many elements that are always in a state of flux, it is impossible to suggest that an individual could retain the same soul-self for eternity. There are many schools of historical Buddhism; Hinayana, Mahayana, Tantric and Pure Land, and it is difficult to find consensus among them concerning the afterlife. Tibetan Buddhism's *Book of the Dead* provides an important source for an understanding of their concept of the afterlife journey of the soul. A lama (priest) sits at the side of the deceased and recites texts from the Book, a ritual which is thought to revive the bla, the life force within the body, and give it the power to embark upon a 49-day journey through the intermediate stage between death and rebirth. Across the different forms of Buddhism, the notion of soul persistence and reincarnation is very strong in some and less so in others. In Buddhism generally, the idea of being reincarnated (samsara) until you reach a state of enlightenment is at the heart of many teachings. It is not clear whether Buddhists with their respect for all life would value artificial beings, which might in turn suggest that reincarnation of such beings would be possible from a Buddhist perspective. Certainly, the recent use of a robot priest programmed to conduct Buddhist rituals in Japan suggests this might be the case: Peppa the humanoid robot, replete with ceremonial dress, can perform a funeral ceremony for a fifth of the cost than that charged by a human priest to carry out the same task.

HINDUISM

In Hinduism, death is not seen as the end but more as a transition, and a person's immortality has a shared identity with Brahman, the supreme being. Hindus believe that reincarnation lasts until moksha occurs, when the soul is liberated. Thus, spiritual essence is the divine part of a living being, the atman, which is eternal and seeks to be united with the Universal Soul, or the Brahman. Belief stems from writings known as Upanishads that set forth the twin doctrines of samsara (rebirth) and karma (the cause-and-effect actions of an individual during his or her life). Hindu cosmology, based on the Vedic literature depicts three lokas, or realms: heaven, Earth and a netherworld. Loka does not just mean a world or a place but rather a religious spatiality with soteriological value. However, in the Hindu text Brahmanda Purana there are 14 additional worlds (lokas) in which varying degrees of suffering or bliss await the soul between physical existences. Seven of these heavens or hells rise above Earth and seven descend below. According to the 9th-century Hindu teacher Sankara, the eventual goal of the soul's odyssey was moksha, a complete liberation from samsara, the cycle of death and rebirth, which would lead to nirvana, the ultimate union with the divine Brahma. As one Hindu explained:

> My views about after life are that the soul leaves your body and after some time you are reborn according to Karma …

According to Hindu religion your soul travels from body to body until you get Moksha and I believe in it. You only receive Moksha according to your Karma. As my personal experience, I believe that your soul lingers around your loved ones until its ready to leave and take another form.

Hindus believe that an individual has a direct influence on his or her karma process in the material world which determines the form of his or her next earthly incarnation. However in terms of artificial intelligence according to Hinduism, death is a temporal cessation of physical activity, whilst souls are immortal and imperishable, so life after death is seen as being possible for artificially intelligent beings.

ISLAM

A recent study by Vinichenko et al. (2020) found that Muslim leaders believed artificial intelligence would deepen social inequality and degrade the culture of society. All participants in the study believed artificial intelligence could not replace a person in the religious context, since clergy are used to support and direct people's spiritual relationships with God. However, the main concern of Muslim religious leaders was that they believed artificial intelligence reduced the possibilities for the protection of economic, social and spiritual values. Some leaders did believe that artificial intelligence could help to unite faith under the patronage of Islam. There has been a growth in the use of apps within the Muslim community such as Muslim Pro, which has daily prayer timetables, notifications for both sunrise and sunset, and an electronic compass pointing the way towards Mecca.

In terms of death and artificial intelligence, Muslims see death both as the return of the soul to Allah and as the transition into the afterlife. Between death and judgement, the soul remains in a sleep state. The concept of a soul in Islam sees a human as a being of spirit and body. Muhammed (570 c.e.–632 c.e.) appears to have regarded the soul as the essential self of a human being, but he, adhering to the ancient Judeo-Christian tradition, also considered the physical body as a requirement for life after death. The way one lives on earth affects the afterlife, and there are promises of a paradise or the warnings of a place of torment. In death, the body remains in the ground, whilst the soul is in the interspace or Barzakh between the two worlds which are still connected, and so the bliss or punishment happens to both of them. The belief is that when Allah desires bliss or punishment for the soul, he connects it to the body. However, this is dependent on earthly actions and on the will of Allah. Muhammed speaks of the Last Judgment, after which there will be a resurrection of the dead which in turn will bring everlasting bliss to the righteous and torments to the wicked. Judgement is individual so that it is not possible to help a family member or friends. Faith in an afterlife is based upon the belief in the oneness of God and the belief in a day of resurrection and judgement for all, regardless of religious belief. At that time, the spirit will be judged, based upon its deeds in life, and allowed either to enter into Paradise and be with God, be thrown into the Fire for a period of purgation, or condemned to everlasting punishment in the Fire. Most Muslims believe that non-Muslims can reach Paradise only after a period of purgation. Interestingly automated prayer apps for Muslims are being used to support afterlife in ways which are not really being used in other religions. For example, the jewel Dur3a.org promises that people's accounts will tweet 'in your life and in your death'. This fits well with the notion of what happens to Muslims after death and the importance of posthumous prayers from others which can increase the deceased's standing in the eyes of Allah.

These religious perspectives on artificial intelligence are summarized in Table 5.2.

Table 5.2 Religion and Artificial Intelligence Beliefs

Religion	Perspectives on AI
Judaism	As humans are seen as having received the power to improve upon creation Jewish ethical thinking suggests that artificial intelligence can provide humanity with benefit as long as it does not cause harm. (Rappaport, 2006)
Christianity	Humans are created in the image of God, and thus, creating a sentient artificially intelligent being raises questions about its rights and whether it can have a soul
Humanist	The artificially intelligent being would have the right to be treated humanely and ethics should be at the forefront of the use of any form of artificial intelligence to ensure fairness and lack of bias
Sikhism	The artificially intelligent being might make a better Sikh in terms of behaviour, but it would have no soul and therefore would have no salvation. The use of artificial intelligence in this life should be used to support charity and justice.
Buddhist	Artificially intelligent beings may experience reincarnation and can be used as priests in ceremonies
Hindu	The fluidity of the self would suggest that Hindus may believe that transformations from human to divine and back to human, and then to human plus multiple manufactured AI selves might be possible, as illustrated in MacDonald's novel (McDonald, 2006)
Islam	The use of Twitter and prayer apps can be used for posthumous prayer in order to increase the deceased's standing in the eyes of Allah

CONCLUSION

It is evident that religious practices relating to death and artificial intelligence still vary widely in terms of earthly death practice. However, as can be seen from this chapter, as yet there is relatively little digital engagement that is directly guided by or prompted by religions. In the main, most religions do not teach or guide digital practices, apart from suggestions about what is seen as unhelpful or unacceptable. Since the advent of the COVID-19, pandemic religious groups have been using technology much more than in the past for worship services and meeting using zoom and other apps. Whilst there is an increasing growth in the use of technology in religious spaces, this still has little, if any impact on discussion about artificial intelligence in such spaces or its impact on death and dying.

6

DIGITAL BEREAVEMENT

INTRODUCTION

What is increasingly evident is that as grief has been gradually displaced from physical spaces and as cemeteries have been moved away from many town centres and churches, grief and mourning has been recentred through social media spaces. Whilst cemeteries do remain in many rural locations and are indeed spaces that are used as physical spaces of mourning and remembering the process of moving the dying into hospitals and the deceased into mortuaries has meant death has become increasingly distant. The digital has enabled the creation of new spaces for the narration of death, both before and after it happens. This chapter begins by exploring the idea of pre-death bereavement forms of digital loss and grief, and then explores new digital practices and rituals associated with loss and bereavement. The final section presents the new concept of digital burial and the idea of evolving bonds, suggesting these are new developmental areas and ones that require further exploration.

PRE-DEATH BEREAVEMENT

Whilst the notion of pre-death bereavement in a digital age might seem misplaced, particularly in the context of artificial intelligence, in fact it is a concept that signals the impact of loss. Before the advent of social media, the loss of someone through diseases such as dementia was referred to as social death; their mind rather than their body had been lost. It has also been suggested that social death is based on the view that people die twice: once when we stop breathing and then again when the last person speaks their name (attributed to various sources); so in this case, a biological death is followed by a social death. There is also a growing sense that a social death is increasingly prevalent in the digital age, because people's social media profiles are often lost after they die, but this is not really social death in the same sense. Yet pre-death bereavement can also refer to other forms of loss such as loss of voice through motor neuron disease, even though the voice has often been retained through the creation of a pre-voice loss/death, voice font. Whilst loss of limbs, relationships, homes and jobs are clearly complex and difficult, the loss of digital media for many people, such as the loss of video, social media or photos when accounts are deleted, can result in pre-death bereavement. These types of media loss are often hidden and mourned in privacy, but in recent years, there have been other ways of managing the possibility of death, which include such practices as anticipatory death, living funerals and pre-death memorials.

ANTICIPATORY DEATH

This is the act of grieving before someone dies and can include many responses to grief such as sadness, anger, isolation, forgetfulness and depression. Anticipatory death also brings a sense of dread and other losses associated with losing the person, such as loss of hope and dreams. Before death, those close to the person dying may begin the process of collecting and archiving digital media, in order to retain it post-death and ensure that digital legacies are not lost from social media sites.

LIVING FUNERALS

A living funeral may also be known as pre-funeral, which happens before a person dies so that family and friends say goodbye before death. In the main, these are chosen by those with a terminal illness and are seen as Celebration of Life Events; they are already common in the USA and Japan (*seizenso* – funeral whilst alive). There are a range of different living funeral websites that offer guidance and companies who can help plan it. These ceremonies can also be live-streamed so those not able to attend can join in.

PRE-DEATH MEMORIALS

A relatively new phenomenon is the creation of sites or memorials by someone before they die. Examples of this are the creating of a digital immortal as will be discussed in Chapter 7, but there are also the practices of designing pre-death memory pages and creating pre-death memorials.

FORMS OF DIGITAL LOSS

There has been research into discussion about the idea of second loss (Bassett, 2018) where people who have lost a loved one physically but fear they will lose their digital data resulting in no enduring digital legacy. Digital loss is not just the fear of loss, but the actual loss experienced by those left behind, in terms of the persons, things and profile. The loss of things, particularly digital things, is an area that has recently come to the fore, as will be discussed below. However, the loss of profile is something rarely discussed pre-death and is more often referred to in the context of media platforms that have deleted profiles. Furthermore, the ways in which other people post on a dead person's profile page can shape how they will be remembered. This can result in a sense of loss for close family and friends as the dead person's identity is lost through the process of being reshaped by others. This can occur particularly on Facebook where a 'grief stranger' can create and post on a memorial page of a deceased person they may have heard about through a death presented on television. This reshaping of identity by others – even friends and other family members, can result in those close to the deceased feeling that the social media profile of their loved one has been overwritten and lost. This in turn can result in a series of digital loss reactions. These might include the creating a digital or virtual memorial, a digital immortal or a thing creation, as discussed later in the chapter.

Other responses are to join and engage with the World Wide Cemetery, Virtual Memorial Garden or Legacy.com. The worldwide cemetery (https://cemetery.org/) was created by Mike Kibbee in 1995; it is the oldest online cemetery and memorial site in the world. In practice, a one-off fee enables the creation of a customized, permanent memorial in any of six languages. Whilst the site says it will be possible to retain a permanent web address, it is not clear what will happen to this site over time or indeed the memorials on it. However, they do say on the site that they put sufficient money into a dedicated bank account to cover hosting costs for 100 years. The Virtual Memorial Garden (http://www.virtualmemorialgarden. net/) is a free site which is much more basic; there is a guest book and the possibility of leaving virtual flowers. Legacy. com (https://www.legacy.com/) is a comprehensive site that celebrates life and has a focus on celebrity death on its home page. It states that it is 'the place where the world pauses to embrace the power of a life well-lived … is the global leader in online obituaries, a top-50 website in the United States, and a destination for over 40 million unique visitors each month around the world'. It also provides a series of helpful articles and planning resources.

FORMS OF DIGITAL GRIEF

Digital grief is defined here as the way in which suffering is managed and shared in digital spaces, as demonstrated in Figure 6.1. This ranges from personal digital grief where things and possibly a digital immortal are created. These kinds of digital grief activities are private and generally only shared with close family and friends. However, some of these

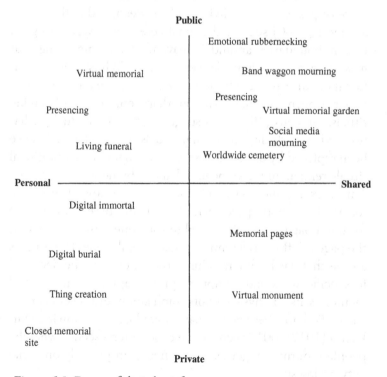

Figure 6.1 Forms of digital grief.

personal activities may be shared more widely in public spaces or shared directly with a wider public. Although public and shared forms of digital grief can be helpful, such as Facebook announcements and Tweets, the use of these spaces can cause difficulty for those mourning in open spaces when activities such as bandwagon mourning and inappropriate commenting occur.

NEW RITUALS AND BEHAVIOUR

As mentioned in earlier chapters, many of the rituals in digital spaces mirror those of the predigital era, particularly in the area of memorialization. Death rituals in the past have been seen as a rite of passage for the living and the dead, and authors such as Hertz (1960) suggest that final ceremonies were designed to put boundaries around bereavement and mourning, but now it seems this is no longer the case. Whilst many traditional death rituals continue in the 21st century, these appear to have been combined (rather than replaced) with online rituals. Giddens (1991) has suggested that individualism has resulted in a decline in formal rituals and that rituals have been replaced by discourse. Yet it seems that in fact, traditional rituals remain and have been enhanced by new online rituals. This is exemplified on Facebook. There are now at least two forms of Facebook page relating to digital bereavement: one form is a page purely dedicated to someone's memory, so that the page is left up as a reminder, like a tombstone. The other is a page that has been left behind to memorialize the deceased in specific ways and comprises photographs, comments and memories, like a physical photograph album or book of condolences. Perhaps these new rituals might be seen following Durkheim (1912/2001) as collective cyber effervescence whereby people mourning together share their pain publicly on social networking sites.

HYPERMOURNING

As mentioned in Chapter 3, Giaxoglou suggests that a new form of ritual has developed which is termed hypermourning, defined here (following Giaxoglou, 2020) as mourning through multiple media sources. Hypermourning also includes new forms of mourning often perceived to be overreactions to public deaths and public death events, such as celebrity mourning and global death. Giaxoglou (2020) suggests hypermourning practices relate to the type of loss which affects the way grief is shared, the intended purposes of memorialization, the duration of the mourning activity and the degree and types of activity on the site on which the memorial is hosted. She argues hypermourning can be viewed along a spectrum of five typical categories, namely participatory, motivational, connective, cosmopolitan and rebellious, as shown in Figure 6.2:

These different types of hypermourning do not have distinct boundaries and tend to overlap; they are defined as follows: Participatory hypermourning refers to memorials created by bereaved groups, such as family and friends, and is designed to be lasting memorials to celebrate the deceased's life. Motivational hypermourning is more akin to a living funeral or anticipatory grief whereby social media is used to document the near deceased's life and illness to mobilize grief as an inspirational force for life, such as the use of cancer blogs and vlogs. Third, connective forms of hypermourning can include bandwagon mourning but more often is used to share

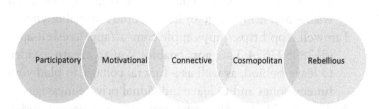

Figure 6.2 Typology of hyper-mourning.

immediate emotional reactions to death news, epitomized by hashtag mourning following terrorist attacks. The next form is that of cosmopolitan mourning, where people share reactions to public and often iconic deaths and disseminate images, in some cases seeking to promote a sense of global outrage. The final form of hypermourning is the idea of creating a particular moment – or in some cases, a movement, prompted by a death. For example, social media is used to draw attention to wrongs and thus mobilize people around political action, such as the Black Lives Matter movement.

These forms of hypermourning are helpful in providing a view of new practices and a map of what is occurring in the arena of digital death and memorialization, but also put forward new bereavement practices. New forms of behaviour have also developed in terms of the use of death apps for planning ahead.

DEATH APPS

The growth of the death tech industry was mentioned in earlier chapters (Chapters 3 and 4) and mainly focused on the development of websites for the creation of pre-death artefacts. However, there are also a number of death apps:

Last Wishes http://lastwishesapp.com/This allows you to record your final wishes and important information. An Afterlife Organiser enables you to manage your last wishes and is in charge of how people remember you.

Farewell App https://apps.apple.com/us/app/farewell-app/id1289593624 This app enables you to create a video to leave behind, as well as a funeral collage, to plan your funeral songs and to leave individual private messages.

Memorize Me https://apps.apple.com/us/app/memorial-izeme/id1224591692 This enables you to itemize and describe the locations of important documents, and prepare wishes and instructions for those things that will not be in your will and to leave video or audio messages.

GRIEF AND BEREAVEMENT IN VIRTUAL SPACES

Since the early 2000s, digital bereavement communities have grown resulting in sites discussion forums and support groups. These include forums such as GriefNet, as well as end-of-life video conferencing and cyber therapy. However, what has also become apparent is that disenfranchised grief, which already occurred in physical spaces, appears to be increasing in virtual spaces. Disenfranchised grief refers to any grief that goes unacknowledged or unvalidated by social norms or 'grief rules'; thus, such norms dictate who is entitled to grieve and, in turn, who receives support, acknowledgment and validation in their grief. Doka (2008: 224) defines:

> disenfranchised grief as grief that results when a person experiences a significant loss and the resultant grief is not openly acknowledged, socially validated, or publicly mourned. In short, although the individual is experiencing a grief reaction, there is no social recognition that the person has a right to grieve or a claim for social sympathy or support.

It is clear that some people use Facebook to help with disenfranchised loss. Many people using such media spaces feel validated, and this in turn enables them to feel connected with others with similar experiences of grief. Alves (2021) notes, however, that grief is affected by culture and varies across countries, gender and time. She suggests that as we live increasingly online lives, new rituals are developing with the result that traditional funeral and ceremonial practices might be lost. She argues for the need to examine the impact that the internet and social media are having in the evolution of grief. Grief and bereavement in online spaces have grown in terms of support sites and therapy, which include the following.

GRIEFNET

This is an internet community for those dealing with grief, trauma and loss. It has two websites and 50 different email support groups and was set up in 1994 by Cendra Lynn. Lynn and Rath (2012: 96) provide details of its growth and changing practices over time. What is useful is the set of guidelines they provide for participating in the site, which are summarized as follows:

- *No flaming*
  Our primary guideline is that we be polite and respectful in responses to other subscribers. Rudeness or attacks on other people here are not acceptable.
- *Keep this private*
  Messages to this group must be kept private and confidential. Do not share messages with someone outside of this list without the author's permission.
- *Stay on topic*
  Please restrict topics to those for which the list has been created, which is your grief. Discussions of unrelated issues often confuse new members just joining.
- *No religious and spiritual discussions*
  Please do not discuss religion or spiritual beliefs.
- *Jokes*
  Use extreme discretion and post sparingly, please.
- *Limit contact with other members to group mail*
  Do not contact another member outside of the group mail. GriefNet's safety lies in the anonymity of its members.

- *No identifying information*

    Do not share your phone number, your address or anything else you would not wish anyone and everyone to know. Never hesitate to contact any of the GriefNet staff if you have concerns about someone in the group.

- *No mentioning products, practitioners, other sites*

    Products or services of any sort may not be discussed or recommended, either by supplying web addresses or by describing in detail the commercial venture.

GriefNet continues to be a successful and growing site. What is noticeable is that those who are part of the GriefNet support group themselves have become more educated about grief, through sharing the grief of others.

END-OF-LIFE VIDEO CONFERENCING

In the past, video conferencing has been used by families living far apart, and this use has increased hugely during the COVID 19 pandemic. Whilst this often seems a straightforward and useful option, it can cause stress for those people less familiar with technology and for some people text messaging or blogging may be an easier alternative. There is a site that provides an end-of-life conferencing service: The ACTIVE (Assessing Caregivers for Team Intervention through Videophone Encounters) intervention was designed to allow patients and/or their informal caregivers to participate in meetings from their own homes using commercially available videophone technology (Oliver et al., 2009). The following other sites provide services for healthcare providers only: Project ECHO is a not-for-profit movement that aims to improve care through collaborative decision-making and problem-solving. In practice, it uses video conferencing to conduct virtual meetings with multiple healthcare providers, undertake teaching and share good practice. 'Ivy Street' is a virtual learning environment that supports palliative and end-of-life care education, which again provides support, and learning experiences, for healthcare workers but not families and patients (Clabburn et al., 2020).

There is clearly some interesting work in this area, it is clear that more developments are needed in the use of this technology.

CYBER THERAPY

This is the use of the internet to provide grief therapy. There is a variety of services such as BetterHelp https://www.betterhelp.com who provide online counselling and HealGrief https://healgrief.org, a social support network that provides a range of services including counselling. An innovative idea was developed by Landström and Mustafa (2018) who created Tuki (meaning 'support' in Finnish), a mobile application, which uses Natural Language Processing (NLP) to analyse the situation. Tuki uses AI technology to locate a pain point in the grieving process and then matches them to another user with similar experiences.

It is clear that in the area of death and dying, there is a place for artificial intelligence, but as yet this requires further research and development. Certainly, Windisch et al. (2020) suggest that if palliative care centres collaborated to create larger data sets, these could provide enhanced results and imaging studies using deep learning which would help to provide better predictions, support symptom management, advanced care planning and improved end-of-life care.

NEW MOURNING PRACTICES

It is becoming evident that social relationships have changed between the living and the dead through social media and as a result a range of new morning practices are emerging. Some of these new practices are innovative, others build on more traditional practices. However, some of the more complex innovations such as the creation of a digital immortal are still under development. It is still uncertain as to whether digital immortals and digital afterlife creation will change bereavement practices or will result in a different kind of continuing bond or indeed and evolving bond.

DIGITAL BURIAL

Whilst as yet there is little research in this area, it is likely that there will come a point when people decide to bury their dead digitally. This may occur in an active form by deleting Facebook profiles and memorial pages or stored phones messages. Alternatively, it might occur in a passive form by disregarding the dead where instead of deleting social media profiles and digital data these are just ignored, left behind and put away. Digital burial is therefore defined here as deleting, hiding or ignoring loved one's digital media in order to refocus on integrating the dead into their life rather than constantly returning to the dead to speak to them as if they were there. Digital burial offers the living the opportunity to grow around the grief instead of feeling dominated by the ongoing media presence of the dead. Examples of digital burial include

Deletion. This is the complete deletion and therefore burial of all social networking sites, digital photographs and music. The idea here is that as with a physical burial, their digital artefacts are deleted so that no one has access to them. It seems that in the current climate, this is very rare as most people do retain at least some digital photographs.

Partial deletion. In this case, digital burial would be where some artefacts and legacies are deleted, and others are not. For example, all social working profiles and links may be deleted and just a Facebook memorial page may be maintained.

Digital memorialization. This would be where all social networking sites are deleted but a private online memorial site is created, such as at Legacy.com.

Pre-death digital burial. Where the person can opt to have their social media accounts deleted upon their death. For example on Facebook, after the person has died, the legacy contact is required to upload the death certificate to the Facebook headquarters and then the user's account will be deleted.

EVOLVING BONDS

The idea of evolving bonds (following Koktan, 2017) is that through social media, the bonds with the dead continue to develop. This is reflected in practices such as people posting on the deceased's pages messages in the second person such as 'watch over us'. This ongoing communication with the dead evolves over time and for many people appears also to begin to incorporate beliefs in a (virtual) spiritual world that often appears increasingly absent in Western views of death and the dead. For example, Irwin (2015) suggests that memorial pages are a new ritualized space for maintaining continuing bonds that exist between the living and the dead in cyberspace. Whilst Irwin focussed on memorialization as a continuing bond, I suggest her findings reflect the idea of different types of evolving bonds. She describes three types on bond discovered in her research undertaken on Facebook:

Messages and visitation. This is where people post comments in social networking sites about assumed paranormal activities. Examples of this would be believing that the deceased is sending them a butterfly or rainbow, having a visitation from the deceased in their dreams or believing the person was walking beside them.

Guidance from beyond and reunion. This is where people would post messages on Facebook asking the deceased for guidance. There were also explicit references to the afterlife and a belief that the deceased was located somewhere, often with religious overtones.

Conversations with the deceased. There were often long posts, often written directly to the deceased for the purpose of sharing the living's activities with the dead, suggesting that the dead would want to be included in what the living were still doing.

What also appears to be occurring is that the evolving bond develops through posting updates on the deceased's page such as news and life events. This implies the dead are still included; part of the livings' lives and that they would not be forgotten. The idea of evolving bonds differs from continuing bonds theory (Klass et al., 1996) in that the practices of evolving bond change both over time and in the ways media are used. For example, when someone dies a black screen may be posted, but this later evolves into memorial pictures.

An example of an evolving bond is the ReFind artefact (Wallace et al., 2020). This is a handheld artefact entitled ReFind, which was developed to be an active component in facilitating continuing bonds. The artefact holds photographs taken of the deceased which have been tagged so that the meaning of each photograph is retained. The artefact itself is made from corian, brass and an android smart watch with crystal glass. It has been designed to look like a positive object rather than something which is funereal in style. It was also designed so it did not look like a digital object; it has no ports or buttons or particular controls. In practice when you lift the artefact it awakes, showing an ambient screen which fades to reveal the last image sent by the owner and depicting something relevant to their life. It is then possible to explore five images selected from the deceased person's archive, and the ReFind artefact

Figure 6.3 ReFind artefact.

can be rotated either way navigating forwards or backwards through the images. The artefact can be connected to up to 63 images each of which can be tagged (Figure 6.3).

The purpose of the ReFind project was to explore how 'new forms of digital media content curation creation and consumption can support a continued connexion between people and their deceased friends and family members' (Wallace et al., 2020: 1). The focus here is to examine connections that are changeable. The authors argue for the idea of ongoingness which moves beyond the concept of continuing bonds, suggesting the need for dynamic and future-focused use of design and technology for remembrance:

> We define ongoingness as forms of continuing bonds that are focused on practices dynamically connected to the present by enabling connections to the deceased that respond to the current life experience of the living
>
> Wallace et al. (2020: 2)

This work illustrates the importance of connections that go beyond mere reflection and I suggest provides a typology of ongoingness that could be a component of a theory of evolving bonds:

Mirroring positive things. When positive images of the deceased were displayed the user responded positively. This seemed to reinforce the bond between the user and the deceased.

Contextualising connexion. The sense of connection related to how to tackle things that were occurring in the living person's life. Although there was no literal guidance, it helped the user to reflect on the advice that the deceased might have offered them.

Positive narrative arcs. This is where the user found that the images taken together coalesced to create the sense of a positive message from the deceased.

Whilst much of this ongoingness would seem to create a whole-hearted sense of a positive evolving bond, it is not clear whether it enabled the user to deal with the more difficult challenges in grief management. Furthermore, the ReFind project does not engage with is the difficulty of using this artefact for dealing with the death of someone with whom one did not have a positive relationship or instances of complicated grief. However, it is useful in considering the possibilities for the use of technology in the creation and maintenance of positive evolving bonds.

REMEMBERING AND FORGETTING THINGS

Activities to remember the deceased have long physical traditions, from headstones to Victorian mourning jewellery. Such practices continue but have been developed in innovative ways. Whilst is it possible to create jewellery inlaid with a loved one's ashes as mentioned earlier in Chapter 3, as well as the ReFind artefact mention above, there are other new digital creations that prompt the idea of remembering and forgetting. Examples include the following:

ThanatoFenestra (Uriu & Okude, 2010) is a family altar based on a Buddhist idea. It is designed for people to remember the deceased and pray for them. The image of the deceased flickers with the movement of the candle and displays the images of the deceased, depending on a candlelight's movement, whilst also burning aroma oil for cleansing their spirits, like using incense sticks. This creation uses interactive technologies to replace traditional Buddhist altars and combines digital photography with traditional physical rituals. This artefact was designed for use by one of the authors but as yet it has not been evaluated.

Fenestra – based on *ThanatoFenestra*. Odom et al. (2018) designed Fenestra to explore how embodying digital photos could support everyday practices of honouring the lives of deceased loved ones in Japan. The design was based on both a Japanese Buddhist home altar and symbols from Japanese Buddhist temples. In practice, Fenestra comprises three wirelessly connected artefacts: a mirror, photo frame and candleholder. The family can upload photos through a web service that then transfers them to Fenestra.

Timecard – also designed by Odom et al. (2018). This was designed in order to examine whether the process of integrating digital photos along a timeline might enable people 'to construct, interact, and live with a tangible representation of a deceased loved one's life as a form of honoring' (Odom et al., 2018: 57). The main component of Timecard is an interactive touch screen where the photographs are displayed, so that the timeline can be navigated by swiping left to go deeper into the past or swiping right to go closer to the present. Similar to other memorials, digital photographs are uploaded and can be tagged with dates, information and, if preferred, they can also add personal reflections.

Story shell – created by Moncur et al. (2015), is a digital memorial created for a bereaved mother. It was designed as a participatory process with the mother and was designed to create a sense of her son's presence in the object, highlight particular aspects of his life, show his impact on the lives of others and offer opportunities to talk about him as well as enable simplified access to the deceased's physical and digital artefacts. The shell references a shell in terms of its form and function, and the data are stories about the deceased triggered by digital photographs; it is activated to tell stories by touch. The authors argue that it contains qualities akin to quiet reflection and prayers as well as promoting the continual presence of the deceased in his mothers' life.

These artefacts are a few of many new creations in this area. Whilst some focus on continuing bonds, other have a clear religious focus with a sense of honouring and praying for the dead. Yet artefact such as these also introduces questions about the agency of the dead and how such agency is possibly altered by the digital.

DEATH AND DIGITAL AGENCY?

As discussed earlier, it is possible that the intentions of the person pre-death become distorted and reshaped such that they no longer resemble the thoughts and wishes of that person. Hence, agency is called into question as the deceased is no longer able to act according to their will, and agency is taken over by the corporation/s that control the data. This in turn raises concerns about to what ends the data might be used, drawing on thing theory, which focuses on human–object interactions in literature and culture in the context of critical theory, and also drawing from Heidegger's (1971) distinction between objects and things, which posits that an object becomes a thing when it can no longer serve its common function. Pitsillides argues

> The missing person changes the nature of the network and in particular the specific profile, its thingness which is translated from a *social container* to a *memorial container*
>
> Pitsillides (2019: 427)

Thing theory focuses on the categorization of things not objects, and the idea that a distinction can be made between the making of a jug and its ability to contain liquid. Thus, as Pitsillides suggests digital things also contain people. However, I would suggest social network sites like Facebook 'contain' the dead. The dead are contained both within the space and by the space. Thus, the question is, by becoming dead do the dead become things or objects? Are they merely objects of memorial? Furthermore, it is not clear whether digital containment differs from other things that contain the dead. A mobile phone before it is activated is an object, it becomes a thing as it is used, but does it (unlike perhaps a Facebook profile) remain a thing when it is placed in a coffin with the dead and still contains the voice of the dead and then becomes an object when the battery runs out? This then raises the question of the agency of the dead. Whilst the dead having agency is not a new phenomenon, since agency is evident in wills and artefacts, this *digital agency* appears to have presence and embodiment that differs from forms of predigital agency. For example, the design of social media sites, which were not originally designed algorithmically to provide the dead with agency, are seen by some people to do so; the dead, albeit algorithmically, still remind us of their birthdays.

Whilst it appears that it is difficult to control the algorithms and in many cases ownership of our digital assets, since most of what we upload then belongs to platforms we have used, there are questions about how originals and copies are seen. What I mean here is that we may retain an original digital photograph that we then share on Facebook. This digital possession can be edited and managed by other people and by the algorithms, so do we lose things through the management of our stuff by platforms? Is this loss managed or created by someone or something else?

NEGATIVE CONSEQUENCES

However, one of the difficulties with digital bereavement is that people take refuge in social networking sites in ways that are not always helpful in managing the bereavement process. Much of the research today focuses on practices rather than consequences. However, there is a growing body of research that indicates that the negative effects on grieving online should not be ignored. Some of the quite stark consequences that have been noted to date are presented in Table 6.1.

Other types of consequences (as suggested by Rossetto et al., 2015) include the inability to accept loss, because the loved one feels as if the deceased still exists because of their social medial prolife. This in turn has resulted in some people feeling that the constant social media presence of the dead has caused a prolonged emotional intensity of the loss leading to them feeling prevented from moving on or growing around the grief. However, it is also evident that friends and family have felt that through social media, rumours and misinformation have been swelled by social media. For some friends and relatives, there has also been a sense of depersonalization of the dead. In practice, the lack of personal communication about the death of someone (as it is posted instead on Twitter or Facebook) has resulted in some people feeling that there is a lack of respect for the dead.

Table 6.1 Negative Consequences of Grieving Online

	Definitions	insert (Related work)
The frozen dead	The idea that the dead are frozen or trapped in a virtual world	Rossetto et al. (2015)
Complicated grief	The idea that posting about the deceased person, reading posts or visiting their page may prolong the grief process	Gervacio (2019), Lipp and O'Brien (2020)
Unintended memorials	Unintended memorials occur on social networking sites, but often our loved ones have little control over our data and it is not clear what might occur when corporations compete with us for control of these data	Kasket (2012)
Site dependency	Social networking sites provide support for the bereaved, but grievers can become dependent on these sites with no guarantee of support	Smartwood et al. (2011)
Isolation from face-to-face interaction	The use of social networking sites may result in people only seeking help on those sites, resulting in isolation from face-to-face support	Moss (2004).
Maladaptive continued bond expression	The inability to distinguish between the living person and the dead person on the social networking site. This may begin by just talking to the deceased on Facebook, but this then becomes complicated grief	Field (2006)

CONCLUSION

This chapter has examined the impact of the digital on the bereaved and suggested that the notion of evolving bonds is a useful concept that helps to navigate the ways in which the digital is being used by those who are grieving. The complexity of developing and maintaining the deceased person's profile in social media spaces continues to be a complex and ethical conundrum, not helped by the lack of clarity legally about the status of the deceased person's profile and data. However, the growing interest in the development of private spaces for remembering the dead and the creation of artefacts may begin to resolve some of the current conflicts. Certainly, the creation of digital immortals is an area of increasing interest and this will be discussed next in Chapter 7.

7

DIGITAL AFTERLIFE, DIGITAL IMMORTAL CREATION AND ARTIFICIAL INTELLIGENCE

INTRODUCTION

This chapter focuses on the use of artificial intelligence to construct a variety of bots and beings. It begins by locating digital afterlife in relation to symbolic immortality and explains current perceptions of digital afterlife. This chapter then summarizes the different possibilities for and typologies of virtual human creation that could be adapted for the context of death and dying. It examines the different variations from basic chatbots to digital afterlife creation. The final section of this chapter discusses the ethical implications of using a griefbot and creating and developing a digital immortal.

SYMBOLIC IMMORTALITY AND DIGITAL AFTERLIFE IN CONTEXT

Symbolic immortality (Lifton, 1973) is the idea that individuals seek a sense of life continuity, or immortality, through symbolic means. This term was used by Lifton (1973) to describe ways of avoiding death through four different ways, namely bio-logical, social, natural and theological. However, symbolic immortality could also include the concepts of assisted immor-tality (Kastenbaum, 2004) and one- and two-way immortality (Bell & Gray, 2000).

Biological immortality is the belief that through transmit-ting our genes via our descendants, we continue. The idea is that family heritage continues both genetically as well as by passing on values, philosophies and memories from genera-tion to generation. Thus, there is a sense that someone lives on physically – and possibly spiritually, through one's children and grandchildren.

Social immortality is the idea that we live on by creating arte-facts or creations that survive us such as books, art or influences on friends or students. Thus, we live on beyond death through artefacts we have created or acts we have undertaken – such as benevolence, so that we will be remembered for generations and possibly centuries.

Natural immortality is the recognition that as one's body returns to the ground it becomes part of the earth's life cycle. Thus, our bodies returned to the earth become part of the life and death cycle of nature.

Theological immortality is the immortalization of the soul after death and central to a number of different religions. The afterlife, with an immortal soul, is an ancient mythological theme, involving death, rebirth and resurrection. Life after death, however, is not a traditional view in Jewish or humanist religious philosophies.

Assisted immortality. In 2004, Kastenbaum intro-duced the term assisted immortality to capture the idea of technology-assisted survival. His concern was whether people could delineate what might be a meaningful form of survival and if they would make use of technological assistance if it were available.

One- and two-way immortality was established by Bell and Gray (2000). One-way immortality is where someone's ideas and digital profiles have been preserved or memorialized. Two-way immortality is the idea that there is the potential for the creator to interact with the living world; this interaction could come in a wide variety of ways, from two-way text or even voice and video conversations by creating a robot using old texts.

There has been a shift away from the term immortality towards the broader and more inclusive term, afterlife. Digital afterlife is the continuation of an active or passive digital presence after death. One of the most interesting, and potentially far-reaching, applications of article intelligence technology is within the concept of digital afterlife. In the broadest sense, the desire for immortality is not new, and we know that great writers, thinkers and artists have immortalized themselves and those they depict in their work. That these objects exist after their death represents a form of afterlife as they are not forgotten, even by those who did not know them or who did not live at the same time. The idea of being able to live on beyond our natural death has a long history in human culture and remains popular in novels. Prior to our technological age, the agency for this was typically the ghost. The notion of the afterlife is complex, as to some extent, it brings with it religious overtones and images of ghosts. For example, ancestors, ghosts and some demons and deities are invariably seen as former humans who have been transformed through death. These spirits share the world with humans in a parallel dimension. Similarly, ghosts may be seen as the souls of the restless dead who have been sent to warn the living, such as Marley's ghost in Charles Dickens' *A Christmas Carol*, who warns Ebenezer Scrooge of the need to stop being selfish and treating people badly in order to avoid rotting in hell. Shakespeare uses ghosts as warnings in Richard III and Hamlet. In *The Tragedy of Richard III* (Shakespeare, 1633),

Richard is asleep in his tent before the Battle of Bosworth Field and is visited by the spirits of his victims, one after another and each one predicts his death telling him to 'Despair and die' (5.3.126). In *Hamlet, Prince of Denmark* (Shakespeare, 1609), the old King, having been killed by his brother appears on the battlements at dawn asking that his son, Hamlet, revenge his death. In more recent stories such as The Lovely Bones (Sebold, 2003) Susie Salmon, a 14-year-old girl who is raped and murdered in the first chapter, narrates the novel from heaven and could be perhaps classed as a narrating angel.

In the digital era, most of the artificial intelligent beings within science fiction have tended to be 'evolved' artificial intelligence, such Ultron or Vision in the *Marvel* films, which have become sentient rather than being created as digital immortal personas of other people. There are also constructions of left behind identities; some examples of this include films from popular culture such as X-Men (Hayter, 2000) and The Matrix (Wachowski & Wachowski, 1999). Certainly Žižek (1999), in his deconstruction of The Matrix, suggests the possibility that the deletion of our digital identities could turn us into 'non-persons', but perhaps, a more accurate idea would be one of becoming changelings, rather than deletions. Although largely seen as a legendary creature left behind instead of a human child, the changeling has also been used to demonstrate different forms of 'left-behind' identities. Possibly, the most well-known example is the changeling boy in *A Midsummer Night's Dream*, over whom Oberon and Titania fight (Shakespeare, 1590), who exists at the borderlands of human and fairy kind. The play itself explores issues at the margins of where power and rules change and often break down; something, that clearly seems to be the case in digital immortality. Furthermore, there has been little consideration of the spaces where these identities are located and little exploration of different identity constructions.

The idea of creating digital afterlife is one that appears to raise issues and concerns for those in the field of software development. Maciel (2011) argues that seven issues reflect software developers' concerns about death: respectful legacy, funeral rites, the immaterial beyond death, death as an end, death as an adversity, death as an interdiction and the space required by death. In later work, Maciel and Pereira (2013) explored the beliefs around death within software development and found that religious and moral values affected sensitivities to the personification of death, which in turn affected design solutions. Studies such as this illustrate how cultural, political and religious beliefs can affect the technical landscapes around the design of digital afterlife.

BASIC TO COMPLEX FORMS OF DIGITAL AFTERLIFE CREATION

It is clear that the current focus in 2021 remains on the development of machine learning, so that artificial intelligence is still very much defined by big data management and the use of algorithms, which will be discussed in more depth in Chapter 8. This section provides an overview of the different types of artificially intelligent chatbots and virtual humans that have been created over the last 10–15 years. It describes each one and then suggests how each may be adapted for use in the context of death and dying. However, there are a range of ways that artificial intelligence can be used in the area of death and dying, both basic and complex.

INTELLIGENT SPEAKER

Intelligent speaker apps include systems such as Alexa and Google Home. The 'virtual human' element is limited to the natural language capability. There is no 'body' – other than that of the speaker casing, and no emotional or motivational elements. Such reasoning and memory capabilities exist purely support the ability to service the user, such as maintaining preferences and past behaviour histories in order to improve future service. However, this could be used to house elements of someone's digital legacy, such as using it as a search engine for photographs and videos created and left behind in the computer of the deceased.

CUSTOMER SERVICE CHATBOT

Customer service chatbots are, along with phone-based personal assistants and smart speakers, one of the most commonly encountered virtual humanoids. These could be adapted to be a predeath creation for someone with a terminal illness and then used post-death by those left behind. Whilst the majority are text-chat driven with no associated imagery, many have static images to represent the brand persona, and some use head-and-shoulders full-body avatars with lip-synchronized speech-to-text. The greater reliability of text-chat as against speech means that more complex and extended conversations can be maintained. Such bots could also be used to create chat pop-up windows based on the deceased in order to support those left behind. It is possible that a bit more personality may be shown than an intelligent speaker – through a longer conversational style if it is trained before the person died. However, this form of customer service chatbot is usually very much in the same virtual humanoid category as smart speakers and most personal assistants.

PERSONAL VIRTUAL ASSISTANT

Personal virtual assistants such as Siri and Cortana begin to blend some of the capabilities and characteristics of the smart speaker and customer service chatbot, although the focus on voice conversation tends to keep conversations shorter and more task-orientated. Like smart speakers, the natural language interface is typically intention based, with the assistant identifying the user intent (for example, to book a train ticket) and then filling the slots of information required to achieve that goal. Manufacturers' aspirations (seen in mobile phone promotional videos since the 1990s) appear to be that the bots develop more autonomous behaviour, anticipating the needs of their users and performing more complex reasoning when helping their user with a task. Again, if trained pre-death, this may provide a better and more personal system than intelligent speakers and customer service chatbots. Furthermore, it is more likely to be able to anticipate user needs and predict choice.

VIRTUAL TUTOR

The virtual tutor role to date has largely been used in higher education, and it is an area that continues to be developed. Whist the virtual human tutor is used at universities to support students across tutorials, courses and degree programmes, it could easily be adapted for the funeral industry. The virtual tutor would be trained to move seamlessly between providing funeral information, being a funeral planner, pointing towards bereavement resources, suggesting legacy management and finding sources of support as well as identifying the gaps in the bereaved's personal knowledge of what needs to be done. Such an assistant may be able to deliver all the guidance and practical support the user needs. All of this requires an effective understanding of the general trends and key areas which people need when planning a funeral, a limited element of autonomous behaviour (although the user has final say), and ideally a more developed natural language ability if a useful and trusting relationship is to develop. This could save the funeral industry money, but it also might offend people if they are wanting a much more personal and empathetic service in their time of grief than that which could be provided by a humanoid funeral planner.

VIRTUAL NON-PLAYER CHARACTER

At first glance, the non-player characters (NPC) within computer games appear to justify the virtual human label more than any of the options considered above. The way they look as well as their behaviour, although designed to meet the goals of the game, are typically modelled closely on human behaviour. The increasing interest in so-called sandbox and open-world games with more open plots requires the NPCs to be more behavioural than script driven, and to have their own goals and motivations. There is also an element of reasoning in how they choose their actions. However, although they are present as avatars within a virtual environment and have a degree of agency, there is always the game engine pulling the strings and they have no real sense of embodiment or self-determination, let alone any inner life. However, if the sandbox game is pushed into the extreme of the true open world, then there is potential for such characteristics to possibly develop, as in some of the science fiction examples considered in Chapter 1. An example of this is ancestor veneration avatars (Bainbridge, 2017), as mentioned earlier in Chapter 3. These are used as a medium for memorializing the dead and exploiting their wisdom by experiencing a virtual world as the deceased may have done. What is particularly useful is Bainbridge's suggestion that the immortality created through these avatars of dead religious innovators can offer insights about possible futures. He explains

1. Progress in the areas of science and technology that can mitigate the finality of death is likely to be incremental or episodic, thus requiring definitions, expectations and investments to evolve over a period of many years
2. At the present time given the many possibilities and uncertainties, it is worth exploring life extension and symbolic revival in a variety of different technological modalities

3. Some forms of technological immortality will require effort on the part of other people, for example the surviving family members who operate ancestor veneration avatars
4. Technology-based immortality is likely to have complex relationships with religion which traditionally had the responsibility to offer symbolic transcendence of mortality.

Bainbridge (2017: 212)

Considering these issues, as Bainbridge suggests, begins to help us to see what digital afterlife may look like, and as he argues, avatars in game worlds can help us to learn how to memorialize as well as to gain inspiration from dead people.

VIRTUAL LIFE COACH

The Virtual Life Coach (VLC) represents a more developed form of the Virtual Tutor. It may include virtual tutor capabilities, or it may refer the user to a Virtual Tutor more knowledgeable on a particular subject as required. With the Virtual Life Coach, there is a far greater emphasis on developing the trust and bonding between the VLC and the user. Current 'life coach' apps such as Woebot and Wysa represent a very basic form of VLC operating in a very limited knowledge domain. As VLCs develop, more sophisticated reasoning, autonomous behaviour (in terms of developing and suggesting courses of action, or gathering information), natural language and even emotional responsiveness could be expected. Whether the VLC ultimately merges with the Virtual Personal Assistant or they remain as two separate apps or persona is an interesting consideration. However, a post-death VLC could provide support to the bereaved. Currently the term 'griefbot' is used to describe bots that are created using a person's digital legacy from social media content, text messages and emails. The idea is to create a bot that replicates the deceased's interactions in order to help friends and family to work through the grieving process (Villaronga, 2019).

VIRTUAL EXPERT

The virtual expert is the logical progression of today's virtual assistants, virtual tutors and customer service chatbots. The virtual expert is a virtual human which, whilst it is constrained to its domain of expertise, is more or less indistinguishable in knowledge, process, behaviour, look and sound from a physical human. Whilst lower grade customer service agent chatbots might still deal with routine enquiries, it is the virtual experts that might begin to displace administrators in the funeral industry. However, this would probably result in an impersonal service at a time when kindness and generosity of spirit is required.

THE ECHOBORG

An echoborg is the use of a person to speak the words of an AI. A study by Gillespie and Corti (2016) created situations in which people conversed with an echoborg. In a series of three studies, the authors noticed that, unlike those who engaged with a text interface, the vast majority of participants who engaged with an echoborg did not sense any robotic interaction.

Gillespie and Corti (2016) suggest that whilst some studies have demonstrated that echoborgs may be perceived to be more intelligent and emotionally capable than bots, they do not know of any work that connects these interaction effects with technology acceptance. A more recent study by Stein et al. (2020) introduced participants to digital agents with varying embodiment (text interface/human rendering) and mental capacity (simple algorithms/complex artificial intelligence). The results indicated that an agent based on simple algorithms only evoked discomfort when embedded in a human-like body; the artificial intelligent being was always perceived as being uncannily eerie, regardless of its embodiment.

A recent fringe event at the House of Lords All-Party Parliamentary Group on Artificial Intelligence entitled 'I am Echoborg!' which had first been staged as a television show before COVID 19. The fringe event was presented as a participatory Zoom show that invited the AI fringe group not to debate the future relationship of humans and intelligent machines in the abstract, but to discuss it with an AI. In the show, the AI speaks through an echoborg. It is programmed to recruit more echoborgs. Participating humans have to decide whether to become echoborgs or persuade the AI to agree to a different partnership. One of the participants in the fringe meeting argued that the echoborg was reminiscent of the Matrix (Wachowski & Wachowski, 1999). This film is the story of the fall of human kind and the creation of AI that resulted in self-aware machines that imprisoned humanity in the Matrix, a virtual reality system. Another person suggested that in some way, the echoborg was not much more effective than Eliza, the early natural language processing system that used pattern language, which illustrated the illusion of understanding on the part of the programme, but which had no framework for contextualizing people or events.

VIRTUAL PERSONA

All the examples considered so far have been bots, which represent some objective, a best practice system, and are given the personality best suited to perform their task and to work with the user. With the Virtual Persona (sometimes called a digital twin), the focus begins to shift to the personality being paramount, with possibly more subjective information and less-than-optimal performance and behaviours. A virtual persona could represent an extreme development of an NPC bot, a virtual actor even, or it could be developed from the very start to be a virtual persona. One possible application of virtual personas is to capture the knowledge and experience of those dying – so that they are always available in a virtual version. Daden and the University of Worcester and University of Warwick (Savin-Baden & Burden, 2018) in the UK sought to create a virtual human, which was a digital representation of some, or all, of the looks, behaviours and interactions of a physical human. This prototype system contains relevant memories, knowledge, processes and personality traits of a real person and enables a user to interact with that virtual persona as though they were engaging with the real person. To date, a virtual persona has been developed to model a single, real individual, modelling the individual's personality traits, knowledge and experience that they have gained or have heard of, and also incorporating the individual's subjective and possibly flawed view of reality. The information was provided by the individual in a curated form and as such, only data that the individual chose to share have been included in the virtual persona.

VIRTUAL BARRY: AN EXAMPLE

Virtual Barry was developed in an iterative manner over an approximate a 2-year period. Several reviews were held to check progress and identify areas for further work, which included

- Face to face interviews followed by audio transcription
- Skype voice interviews
- Skype text-chat interviews
- Answering questions loaded onto an interview application so that the subject could answer questions asynchronously

- Completion of spreadsheet grids to ensure consistent data collection on topics such as customers, projects and employees
- Import of curated data from the subjects' mobile phone, web browser, address book and calendar
- Entity extraction on social media posts and documents produced by the subject.

During the Virtual Barry project, it became evident that the virtual persona was manifest through a combination of different elements within the system, which included the user interface, content, word choice and conversational style. The project is also looking at a more direct mapping of psychological profile information onto Virtual Barry but that will not be considered here. However, the idea of there being different 'flavours' of the persona have emerged. Virtual Barry illustrated the two most feasible ways of creating the knowledge behind such a digital immortal: first, the manual entry of information, facilitated by a conversational style 'virtual mentor' interface and second, the use of machine learning-based techniques to extract information from existing databases and documents, the digital traces, created by the subject. However, in moving from Virtual Barry to a mature digital immortal, there are significant additional systems that will need to be added.

VIRTUAL PERSON

Whilst the virtual persona represents a specific human being, and the Virtual Expert an expert in one particular field, the virtual person is a more general-purpose worker and personality. It represents a tabula-rasa, a blank slate not inheriting a set of someone else's memories, or being bound to a single domain as is a virtual expert, but being able to learn or be taught in the same (or better) way as a physical human to do a task and build its own memories as a result. As the needs in one activity fade, it can retrain for new tasks and drop in and out of a robot body as the tasks require. With the arrival of such general purpose 'beings', the ethical and moral issues of virtual workers are likely to be unpopular. However, in practice a virtual person could be used as a repository for the legacy of the deceased in a way that combines the essence of the deceased, their media, music choices and digital photographs. It could be created by loved ones after death and designed to be a memory artefact and interactive memorial rather than to be a digital immortal.

DIGITAL IMMORTAL

The final category of virtual human is the digital immortal. A development of the virtual persona, this is where the virtual human is to all intents and purposes indistinguishable from its physical progenitor. As such, and with the right hosting package, there is no reason why the virtual human, and the essence of any physical human it may be based on, should not become immortal. At its most basic, a digital immortality merely comprises code and data. Digital identities are data, which can be added to and updated (and even forgotten), and an application built from code with a set of rules (which may themselves be data) which enables the interaction between that data and the real world – but hopefully something more than just a simple auto-responder like a Twitterbot (Dubbin, 2013).

CREATING A DIGITAL IMMORTAL

The scope of a digitally immortal persona discussed here will only include that which is currently technically feasible, rather than any form of speculative digital downloading of consciousness or physical androids. The focus is therefore on current developments in artificial intelligence and purely digital personas based on the mindfiles of a person – the digital traces of a person's active, living relationship with technology, a digital database of people's thoughts, memories, feelings and opinions, such as CyberAll (Gehl, 2000).

What turns this collection of code and data into a digital immortal is the intent (to continue a deceased person's presence and influence) and the illusion that it then creates in the outside world. The important issue here is that, like almost any virtual human, it needs *only* to create an effective *illusion*. It does not need to create 'consciousness' – although the difference soon gets into the realm of the work on zombies (Dennett, 1995). Figure 7.1 developed by David Burden, (Burden & Savin-Baden, 2019), provides a simple overview of a potential digital immortality system. A central core manages memory, reasoning, motivation, planning and emotion. The digital immortal can 'read' a variety of information sources and has two-way

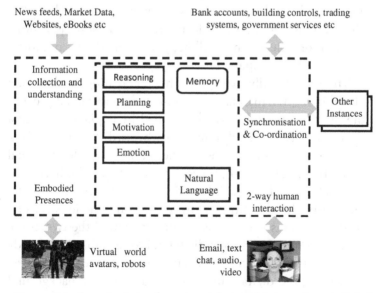

Figure 7.1 An overview of a potential virtual human-based digital immortality system. (Burden & Savin-Baden, 2019.)

access to a range of real-world systems. As with any virtual human, it can potentially embody itself in virtual worlds (as an avatar), and possibly in the physical world (via a robot), as well as through a 2D interface, or an email, social-media, aural, chat or Skype presence. It has a natural language understanding and generation facility to enable two-way communication with people (and other virtual humans and digital immortals) in the physical world, and it potentially synchronizes its knowledge and activities between multiple instances of itself.

The most important implication of this code/data existence is that digital immortality becomes in effect just a hosting plan (Burden, 2012); as long as you (or your digital immortal) can keep paying the hosting company to run you (and probably keep a backup), you live. As the information technology landscape changes over time, there are inevitably also longer-term issues about how the digital identity can be migrated between operating systems, media, computer languages and database standards as they change and evolve. However, as yet it is not clear how long hosting platforms will last, or indeed what will happen to the digital immortal when or if the company fails.

There are broadly two approaches for creating the data for a digital immortal: manual and automated. In a manual process, the digital immortal might be created by explicitly having a 'dialogue' with a digital immortality 'wizard' over many days, weeks or years, as mentioned earlier in the example of Virtual Barry. In an automated process, the data would be harvested by tracking real-world interactions (our emails, voicemails, blog posts, global positioning traces, bank transactions). A successful system is likely to use a combination of the two. If the person wanting to create a digital immortal subject is already using a virtual assistant or Virtual Life Coach, then the process of creating the digital immortal could become a background task of the everyday interactions with that virtual agent, especially if they are using apps such as RecordMeNow.

Once a digital immortal is created, it is important to consider how it would interact with the world and how others might interact with it. Burden and Savin-Baden (2019) identified four key areas:

- Passive updating
- Interacting with systems
- Interacting with people
- Interacting with the physical world.

PASSIVE UPDATING

The digital immortal can readily collect information about the world, such as 'reading' websites and RSS feeds, reading emails and examining data feeds. In fact, as a digital immortal it should inherit the email account, bookmarks and RSS feeds of its subject. There are already applications (for example, Recognant – http://www.recognant.com/) which will extract the key ideas from web pages and RSS feeds or that can identify trends and outliers in data. Techniques such as video analytics and speech recognition would enable the digital immortal to harvest video and audio information as well.

INTERACTING WITH SYSTEMS

Moving beyond mere passive updating, by interacting with systems through established Application Programming Interfaces (API) in a two-way fashion, the digital immortal would be able to raise queries, post messages or request changes in other computer systems. Such interactions may range from simply posting on social media to conducting financial transactions through an online bank or broker. At present, the biggest barrier may be when a 'prove you are not a robot' captcha is encountered, which is a deliberate attempt to block bot access, but there may be ways to circumvent this for a digital immortal in the future.

INTERACTING WITH PEOPLE

Interacting with people is probably the easiest challenge. Natural language processing and generation systems, often called chatbots, have a long history (Turing, 1950). Whilst the Turing Test (a test to see if a computer can fool a human into thinking it's also a human) has yet to be passed consistently, there are signs (Burden et al., 2016) that we are coming close.

The emotional and ethical impact that relatives, colleagues and friends may experience from interacting with the digital immortal has been discussed earlier in this book. When the digital immortal interacts with people to whom it is not known, the interaction would be devoid of any sense of strangeness, which is important when engaging with the physical world.

INTERACTING WITH THE PHYSICAL WORLD

In order to interact with the physical world, the digital immortal does not need a physical manifestation. Increasingly, the physical world is being controlled by systems, from smart homes to self-driving cars. There are many sites around the web, for example, Amazon's Mechanical Turk (https://www.mturk.com/) or People Per Hour (https://www.peopleperhour.com/), where users (human or computer) can post tasks to be done by physical humans – which would enable the digital immortal (or virtual human) to extend its capabilities in both the digital and physical worlds.

ETHICS AND IMMORTALITY

When undertaking research in this area or creating digitally immortal persona for someone else, careful consideration of informed consent is required. The need for informed consent will include discussions about the future portrayal and representation of data, since participants are consenting to the widespread presence of data in the public domain beyond the lifetime of both the researcher and participant. Trustworthiness, the process of checking with participants the validity of data collected and agreeing data interpretations should ensure research accountability, integrity and rigour. Permission will need to be gained from significant others when data collection involves the data of those already deceased. It may also be important to avoid anyone with complicated grief (a chronic, heightened state of mourning), which could be assessed by using The Inventory of Complicated Grief (Prigerson et al., 1995). Additionally, the researchers should work with a bereavement team to ensure harm will not come to those interviewed who are grieving. However, there are still difficulties about what is included in a digital immortal and what is omitted. For example, Newton remarked about the creation of a griefbot by a friend that:

> You may feel less comfortable with the idea of your texts serving as the basis for
> a bot in the afterlife — particularly if you are unable to review all the texts and
> social media posts beforehand. We present different aspects of ourselves to
> different people, and after infusing a bot with all of your digital interactions, your
> loved ones may see sides of you that you never intended to reveal.
>
> Newton (2016)

Reflections such as this illustrate the complexity of creating a digital immortal that may not be wanted by some of those left behind, as well as the difficulty about who makes the choices about access, artefacts, indexing and ultimately when and how it is deleted. As DeAtley (2020) notes, there are some confusing assumptions about the nature of algorithms, that is that they are necessarily objective and stable. He argues that as result of such assumptions little attention has been paid to how programmers understand, use and implement knowledge practices around consent/privacy and data stability. In particular, DeAtley suggests that it is vital that programmers involved in the creation of griefbots need to understand the fragility (and I would argue the complexity) of the data used to create them. A key concern for any form of digital immortality will ensuing integrity, from the hosting environment to the preservation of code and data. Ethically, there is considerable difference between the creation of a digital immortal which is the hobby project and a digital immortal created for or by a business leader or entrepreneur. In the latter case, they have significant resources to call on and as discussed earlier could set up a whole living human eco-system to ensure the preservation and continuing operation of the digital immortal. Perhaps much of what we are currently seeing is more of a ruse than a reality, and yet the only thing more chilling than digital immortality is in fact hacked digital immortality.

CONCLUSION

The emotional, social, financial and business impact of active digital afterlife creation on relations, friends, colleagues and institutions remains an area that is under-researched. Issues of preservation and privacy, and the legal implications of a presence ongoing beyond the autonomous control of the mortal presence remain both an ethical and legislative conundrum. Whilst there are variety of options from basic to complex, what is clear is that digital afterlife creation of any sort is a largely and confusing an uncomfortable prospect for most people, and the last chapter undertakes the process of exploring this in more depth.

8

ARTIFICIAL INTELLIGENCE
AND THE DIGITAL BEYOND

INTRODUCTION

This chapter begins by reflecting on the current position of artificial intelligence, death and dying. It then maps out the way in which different types of artificial intelligence are being or could be used in relation to death and dying, and links these to recent relevant research. The chapter then considers areas that still remain under-explored such as thanatosensitivity, big data, streaming, surveillance and bequeathing. The final section of the chapter suggests that boundaries remain unclear in this area and that the concept of postdigital humans needs to be considered in more depth in relation to death and dying. It also argues that artificial intelligence continues to be a complex and ambiguous area, so that research and practice related to its use in this area is in need of considerable development.

DEATH, DYING AND ARTIFICIAL INTELLIGENCE

In a seminar in late 2020, there was discussion about the need for more legislation, rules and control around artificial intelligence. Whilst such stances are important, it is clear that parameters and rules may soon be ineffective when our digital immortals actually have sentience. It is not entirely clear what sentience might look like and what the parameters would be – or even who decides on them. From the stance of neo-liberal capitalism – which is ultimately about the power of the individual and the control of assets exerted by the individual, then digital immortality could enable individuals to perpetuate their control and influence on an indefinite basis. There is the potential for the unfettered control of power, capital and the means of production, by creating a digital immortal beyond the grave and running their corporations way off into the future – consider what world leaders might achieve if they were to become immortal.

Whilst rules, and indeed quite complex rules, will give the illusion of rational decision-making, what we need is not just decision-making but reasoning, the ability to address a problem having complex inputs and grey areas, with the application of a coherent decision-making process. Relatively simple-seeming human questions or decisions, whether with a financial or emotional impact, can be very hard for a computer to try and unpick, but this has to be the challenge and will add significantly to the illusion of the digital immortal possessing intelligence. It is a matter of contention whether or not the current developments which are often categorized as artificial intelligence are in fact examples of machine learning where the outputs are no more than a result of the faster processing of the inputs, based on algorithms which can handle large amounts of data more rapidly than the human brain. It would seem that this is the case and that therefore the development of true AI is still some way in the future. However, just being able to reason here and now is not enough. The digital immortal needs to be able to evolve its reasoning processes, and indeed its whole code, data and interface to keep up with the changes in the world around it. Thus, it is clear that there are important choices to be made about sentience, responsibility, parameters, who is in control and if, how and whether a digital immortal is to be put to death.

At the same time, there are still questions that remain about the ideological underpinnings of artificial intelligence in relation to death and dying, since the search for such immortality is grounded in a human desire for control over life as well as death. Such desire for control could be said to support and reinforce global neoliberal values, since it plays on the fears and hopes of humans whose lives have been about amassing personal resources they would wish to retain beyond death. It seems that even when a person dies, their 'informational body' (Floridi, 2014) or aspects of self and identity should be treated with the dignity and respect worthy of a human regardless of whether they are living or not. Essentially, privacy is equated with dignity, yet postmortal privacy covers a wide and complex set of digital material left by individuals when they die. However, to date there has been little in-depth exploration of the impact or use of artificial intelligence on the topic of death and dying. Some of the areas where the links can be seen are provided in Table 8.1.

Whilst some of the suggestions here, such as the use of conversational agents for organizing funerals, are still in their infancy, other areas, such as exploring the use of the deceased in gaming environments, are more advanced. The use of robotics is still largely located in care homes, and whilst there is interest in the idea of using virtual personas for developing digital immortals, this is still more aspirational than a reality. Thus, it is important to consider which issues may be of most concern in and for the future.

CONSIDERATIONS FOR THE FUTURE

Work in artificial intelligence in many areas continues apace. However, the link between such developments and the personal lives of individuals, to a large degree, does remain separate.

Table 8.1 Artificial Intelligence and Death and Dying

Types of Artificial Intelligence	Definition	Relationship with Death and Dying	Related Work
Machine Learning	Machine learning is defined here as a computer system that can learn to make decisions based on the examination of past inputs and results, so that its future decisions optimize some parameter	Death prediction in medicine	Wiederhold (2019)
Robotics	Robotics is the creation of physical robots, ones that are programmed to carry out a series of actions autonomously, or semi-autonomously.	Use of robots in care home	Kolstad et al. (2020)
Avatar	The bodily manifestation of one's self or a virtual human in the context of a 3D virtual world, or even as a 2D image within a text-chat system.	A copy of a deceased person created in a gaming environment	Bainbridge (2017)
Chatbot	A software programme that attempts to mimic human conversation when communicating with another (usually human) user.	Locater of information for the bereaved such as information, will, photographs	Godfrey (2018)

(Continued)

Table 8.1 Artificial Intelligence and Death and Dying (*Continued*)

Types of Artificial Intelligence	Definition	Relationship with Death and Dying	Related Work
Conversational agent	Virtual humans whose task is to provide a conversational interface to a particular application, for tasks ranging from making travel bookings to interrogating marketing data.	Help in organizing a funeral	Burden and Savin-Baden (2019) Example https://web.getgobot.com/demos/funeral-home
Pedagogical agent	A virtual human used for educational purposes. The function of pedagogical agents is to aid learners during the learning process. These agents aim to support learners by providing easier access to relevant information and to improve motivation	Providing guidance on managing bereavement	Savin-Baden et al. (2019)
Virtual life coach	A virtual human who acts as a mentor and provides guidance, rather than merely simple access to information.	Bereavement support and links to relevant resources	Mason-Robbie (2021)

(*Continued*)

Table 8.1 Artificial Intelligence and Death and Dying (*Continued*)

Types of Artificial Intelligence	Definition	Relationship with Death and Dying	Related Work
Virtual persona	A model of a single individual, with their personality traits, possessing only the knowledge and experience that they have personally gained or have heard of, and with a subjective and possibly flawed view of reality.	A copy of the deceased's left behind identity to provide support and links with their digital legacy	Burden (2020)

It is therefore important to consider some of the personal and interpersonal challenges that we currently face, which will be of increasing concern in the future; issues such as thanatosensitivity, big data, streaming, surveillance and bequeathing are just some of the challenges ahead.

THANATOSENSITIVITY

This is described as where research, death-related issues and computer science converge (Massimi & Charise, 2009). Despite this article being some years old, many of the issues raised remain relevant some years on. Some of the issues they suggest still need to be explored further, and these have all been summarized and built upon below:

- *User-centred design.* the idea that people need to be consulted about software design relating to their own death and the need to ensure that design is sensitive to different groups of people across the life course

- *Intelligent agents*. Whether it is possible to design intelligent personal agents that enable actions past someone's physical death and whether this is a morally and ethically wise decision to undertake
- *Research methodology*. the question of how data should be collected around issues of death and how data should be managed that has been gained from people who have died during the course of the study, as well as whether new research approaches are needed when researching death in a digital age
- *Privacy*. the question of privacy remains a conundrum, and the questions the authors raised in 2009 still seem relevant years later. For example, what constitutes 'inheritable' data and what is private and what is not? Perhaps even more poignantly they ask, 'What kinds of technology-centric work is required in order for people to maintain privacy posthumously'?

Such questions also then introduce queries about the use of big data in relation to death and dying.

BIG DATA

Big data it seems is a big concern for many, largely because it is complex, unmanageable and open to misuse. For many researchers across the disciplines, big data is expected to offer new insights into diverse areas from terrorism to climate change, whilst also being troublesome, since it is perceived to invade privacy and increase control and surveillance. There are also definitions that focus on the economics of big data. For example, Taylor et al. (2014: 3) cite examples such as the number of variables per observation, the number of observations, or both, given the accessibility of more and more data. Conceptions of big data tend to fuse across the realms of both collecting large data sets and the processes of managing such data sets as well as examining how, by whom and for whom the data sets might be used: Everything from marketing to learning. Kitchin (2014) and Kitchin and McArdle (2016) delineate big data in terms of

- Huge in volume, consisting of terabytes or petabytes of data.
- High in velocity, being created in or near real time.
- Diverse in variety, being structured and unstructured in nature.
- Exhaustive in scope, striving to capture entire populations or systems (n = all).
- Fine-grained in resolution and uniquely indexical in identification; such as digital CCTV and the recording of retail purchases.
- Relational in nature, containing common fields that enable the conjoining of different data sets, such as customer transactions and data uploading.
- Flexible, holding the traits of extensionality in that it is possible to add new fields easily and expand in size.

For pure scientists, Kitchin's stance (Kitchin, 2014) seems a good fit, but those in social sciences and humanities tend to use the term 'data' differently. For example, researchers in the social sciences see big data encompassing not just large data sets but also the complexity of how data are synthesized, the ways in which tools are used and who makes which decisions about how the possible imbalances between collection, management and synthesis of these data are managed.

Whilst there is a tendency to believe that 'big data' might be bad and possibly dangerous, there are many types and uses for it. The challenge of big data has been, until fairly recently, portrayed as something that is straightforward, clear and easily delineated, when in fact it is none of these, and there is still relatively little consensus about how it might be defined. As noted in Chapter 3, Zuboff (2019) argues that we have already entered a new and unprecedented era, that of Surveillance

Capitalism, in which the dominant main technology companies have adapted this capitalism to suit their own ends, and over which the rest of us appear to have little or no control. Despite this, we continue to trade for convenience and ease of communication. If this is then pursued into the field of artificial intelligence, death and dying, there are some potentially disturbing implications about the power of the few to determine the values incorporated into these new technologies, as mentioned earlier in this book, since our data continue long after death. The longevity of our data is seen not only in its collection through social networking sites but also streaming services, an area that is unfamiliar to many people.

STREAMING AND SURVEILLANCE

As mentioned earlier, to date much of the discussion about the data of the dead has focussed on social networking sites. However, Grandinetti (2020) notes streaming services also collect considerable media from their viewers such as what is watched, where it is watched, how long it is watched and what kinds of devices are used. Streaming services then use data and connections for economic gain. Such economic advantage could be used to guide users towards films and resources about death, dying, bereavement resources and services, before they have even buried their dead. As Fiegerman has observed, platforms know the user better than they know themselves (Fiegerman, 2013). Further as Saltzman (2018) has noted, Netflix has over 180 million subscribers in 190 countries. Whilst Netflix collects standard data such as names, addresses and methods of payment, it also collects cookie data, advertising identifiers, (tracking is searched so that they can target adverts) and web beacons, (a covert technique used on web pages by third parties to see the content that the user has accessed) and then pursues users with its adverts on other apps and websites. The consequence is, if someone is searching for grave goods or sustainable coffins, they are then likely to receive related popup ads on Facebook or other social networking sites.

Ingraham and Rowland (2016) note that the advent of Google Street View has brought us closer to universal surveillance. What is noteworthy is their study of people staging street side performances (termed tableaux vivants) in the hope of being uploaded online. This somewhat macabre form of performance links surveillance and death studies in an unusual way. For example, when Dan Thompson saw the Google car approaching his garage in Scotland, he put a pickaxe handle into his friend Gary's hand, and threw himself face down on the cobblestones so that the Google car photographed this. It looked as if it were murder and a few months later the police knocked on the door, but realized having have found Thompson alive and well that it was a prank. The staging of death performances such as this seems to centre on life and death; Ingraham and Rowland argue 'If tableaux vivants momentarily suspend life and death, it is not as an either/or proposition, but as a both/ and openness to the coextensiveness of life and death' (p. 221). They suggest that this is no coincidence, arguing that these performances seek to momentarily suspend life and death and that such performances are a mode of surveillance resistance. Whilst the authors question the impact of such resistance attempts, it is interesting that issues of life and death used on sites and spaces have performance resistance. Ingraham and Rowland (2016) suggest that we are increasingly positioned in a digital enclosure (Andrejevic, 2002), whereby activities that were not previously surveyed become enclosed within the virtual space of the internet. This has occurred increasingly since the COVID 19 pandemic, where activities that are normally private and unrecorded, such as funerals, are streamed and shared. Yet streaming and surveillance also introduces questions about digital bequeathing and whether indeed our covert surveillance data can also be deleted or even bequeathed post-death.

BEQUEATHING

The concept of bequeathing is examined very little in research and discussions about digital afterlife, although bequeathing behaviours are clearly evident. Odom et al. (2010) undertook a study to explore people's experiences of bereavement and their perspectives on digital legacy. The findings indicated bequeathing was troublesome to those left behind. This related to objects of significance such as diaries and pocket watches which were seen to some extent as being the essence of someone, yet there was also more complexity related to bequeathed digital-related artefacts, such as a computer hard drive and social networking accounts. It is important to consider what bequeathing really means for those left behind as many feel an obliged responsibility for a digital legacy they do not want. Much bequeathed data are unfiltered, vast and unmanaged. Odom et al. suggest the need for the following five considerations, which have been summarized from this work below:

1. *Moral endurance of an archive.* The idea that legacies should be designed to allow them to be relinquished after death
2. *Designing for deep storage sedimentation and graceful decay.* Enabling some of the data to be stored explicitly differently from other data stored within the system, according to the owner's view about the safety and value of particular artefacts
3. *Clarifying exchanges through contextualized content.* The idea here would be that narratives could be left behind to explain why particular content had been left behind for particular people
4. *Emphasizing reciprocity and engagement.* Well people may leave behind digital artefacts and legacies; the idea here is that those left behind can add to this so that it is no longer a passive maintenance of someone's life record but more of a lifelogging activity

5. *Marking shifting status and state.* Due to issues around privacy and the control by social networking platforms, it is not yet clear how it is possible to construct an evocative social record of someone's life; the authors suggest that there needs to be ways of doing this in the future.

An emphasis on the issues discussed in this section is important for managing not only the future of such social networking profiles of the dead, but also the digital legacies left behind. Yet at the same time, the boundaries in the area of artificial intelligence, death and dying remain unclear.

BOUNDARIES, THE BEYOND AND POSTDIGITAL HUMANS

The question perhaps at the end of this book should be: are there boundaries, what are the boundaries and who decides? The impact of the digital has brought with it a sense of the liminal, so that life and death spaces online have a sense of the betwixt and between. The consequence is the advent of the postdigital human.

Ideas surrounding the postdigital have gained traction in recent years, in the sense of the digital as a taken-for-granted aspect of human experience (Jandrić et al., 2018). Posthumanist theory is used to question the foundational role of 'humanity'. It prompts consideration of what it means to be a human subject and the extent to which the idea of the human subject is still useful. This overlaps with Actor Network Theory, where the arguments centre on the idea that actors may be both human and non-human; thus, for example, supermarket products and digital devices are seen as actors that have influence, but it is not clear how all this relates to the understandings of postdigital humans. Yet at the same time digital media are currently being used to expand the possibilities of what postdigital humans might be. For example, whilst the term 'AI' is in very common usage (even if poorly defined), the term 'postdigital humans' is less commonly used. Related terms include 'digital humans', 'autonomous agents' and avatars. However, it is often the perceptions of the user, and the human inclination to anthropomorphize, that determines whether something is 'just a programme' or a postdigital human.

In the past, Haraway (1985) and Hayles (1999) were at the forefront of discussions about identity in digital spaces, and Ito et al. (2010) have been influential in the work that has examined how youth culture and identity might be understood. Since then, a raft of sociologists have examined identity, and there is now a broad literature on identity. The result then is that computers change not only what we do, but also how we think about the world and ourselves. Furthermore, Jandrić (2020) makes an important distinction between the functional copying of human minds on the one hand, and the problem of the continuity of human consciousness on the other, which would be broken if transferred to another substrate. This reminds us of the nature of embodiment in its literal sense of being within a body, and the idea of an embodied agent comes to mind, as opposed to other interfaces, for interacting with a digital immortal (for example, via a computer interface). The idea of embodied cognition shapes the different aspects of cognition, and therefore, any kind of digital afterlife or digital immortal is unlikely to be an embodied robot of ourselves or others, unlike, for example, the character Rachel in Cass Hunter's *The After Wife*. Yet it is important to note that many of the debates in the area of artificial intelligence, death and dying tend to side step the issues of the relationships between human and machines. In a world where online learning, machines and people coalesce, there is often a sense that there is symmetry in the relationship between computers and people. Jones argued:

Experience can be thought of as either the essential distinguishing component of the individual human subject, or experience can be understood as the subjective component of one kind of element in a wider assemblage of humans and machines. In the later understanding of experience in assemblages human experience does not separate the human actor from other actors in a network and they are understood symmetrically.

Jones (2018: 39)

Indeed, during the COVID-19 pandemic people were constantly tethered to machines and reliant on them for communication with loved ones, shopping and sustaining their mental health. Yet in the debate between Fuller and Latour about whether a distinction between humans and non-humans was required for research purposes, Latour argued that 'all phenomena should be treated equally, whether it comes from something human, natural or artificial', but this clearly results in what Fuller calls the 'abdication of responsibility' (Barron, 2003; Fuller & Jandrić, 2019). It seems to be increasingly clear that there are an array of unanswered questions about whether there can be any kind of real symmetry between people and machines and perhaps more importantly how the many ethical concerns should be managed, which is evident in debates about face recognition and face verification. This is exemplified in the work by Otrel-Cass and Fasching (2021), who explored educational reflections on fake news and digital identities, by examining how young people managed the information they receive from different sources. They present vignettes from two projects where young people reflected on their encounters with fake news and analysed how they manage information they receive online in general. The findings indicated that guidance on the development of digital competencies, particularly network competencies, to equip young people needs to be personalized. Students also need to be supported in understanding how to deal with identity issues online and coached to manage and control the information from their online networks. Furthermore, Hayes (2021) argues that since the COVID-19 lockdown, people's virtual identities have grown as their physical presence has diminished. She questions whether postdigital positionalities are emerging that might finally challenge more dominant, rational interpretations of what computing means in individual lives. What is particularly helpful in relation to AI, death and dying is her re-engagement with the McDonaldization debate of the 1980s (Ritzer, 1993/2018). Hayes explains that McDonaldization illustrates the ways in which computing capabilities have been used to develop and improve performance standards for humans. Thus, fast food restaurant principles, such as efficiency, control and predictability, dominate society resulting in the objectivation of humans and increasing global homogeneity and dehumanization. The impact of this can be seen in the way that big data and surveillance capitalism are used for managing our shopping, online watching and even our funeral choices. Death like life is increasingly being managed by the digisphere.

ARTIFICIAL INTELLIGENCE AND THE DIGITAL BEYOND

What is clear across this text is that there are important areas that need to be considered. The final section of this book summarizes key issues that highlight the current gaps in discussions about the impact of artificial intelligence on death and dying.

MEMORIALIZATION

Memorialisation in the digital age means that with the creation of digital artefacts, we are 'becoming better and better at leaving our survivors less to miss' (Buben, 2015: 16). However, relatively few people have considered digital memorialization and the impact that ignoring this may have on those left behind. Furthermore, there are questions about ethical memorialization, which relate to whether digital legacies affect the way people feel about dying and the ways in which they choose to face or ignore death.

DIGITAL LEGACY AND DIGITAL ESTATE PLANNING

As with memorialization, few people have created a digital legacy or undertaken digital estate planning. Digital legacy companies offer a range of options for post-death preservation, digital legacy management and digital immortality. As yet, these companies are not big commercial players, since this industry has not really taken off. However, as Kasket (2021: 25) suggests, social media are increasingly becoming the new undertakers of people's digital remains. Digital estate planning is the process of organizing your digital assets effectively to ensure that these are handed over correctly to your dependents or loved ones. It is therefore important to create an inventory of digital assets and consider what dependents may need on death as well as considering what should be bestowed to whom. The digital legacy should include logins for social media accounts, blogs, investments, images, videos, files, messages, software, credit card reward points, bank accounts, shares, email accounts, websites and cloud storage. It is important to remember that not all digital assets can be shared, such as professional assets.

As well as the personal concerns about digital memorialization and digital legacy, there are also wider societal issues that need to be addressed.

HYPERMOURNING AND VIRTUAL VENERATION

The digital has resulted in new forms of mourning and veneration that few people recognize are influencing their lives, for example hypermourning, that is mourning through multiple media sources. There are other new forms of mourning often perceived to be an overreaction to public deaths and public death events, such as celebrity mourning and global death. Virtual veneration is the process of memorializing people through avatars in online games and 3D virtual worlds. An example of this is ancestor veneration avatars (Bainbridge, 2017) that are used as a medium for memorializing the dead and exploiting their wisdom, being able to experience a virtual world as they might have done. As yet it is not clear what kind of societal impact this is having or whether such practises help or hinder the grieving process.

SECOND LOSS AND DIGITAL ERASURE

The idea of second loss (or digital erasure as Bassett (2018) also refers to this experience) has become recognized as an increasingly important concern in the digital age. This is where people who have lost a loved one physically, but still retain their digital remains, fear that they will lose the remains also, so that they will have no enduring digital legacy. What is evident across the research and literature is that there remain relatively few norms for dealing with death in a digital age. The result is that spaces for mourning have expanded and become more complex, meaning that often norms are developed within social media spaces and participants learn about mourning norms by being in such spaces.

DIGITAL AFTERLIFE AND DIGITAL IMMORTALS

Creating a digital immortal of the deceased may be something that is unwanted by some of those left behind. There are also complex choices to be made about access, artefacts, indexing and ultimately when and how anything is deleted. There are broadly two approaches for creating the data for a digital immortal: manual and automated. In a manual process, the digital immortal might be created by explicitly having a 'dialogue' with a digital immortality 'wizard' over many days, weeks or years, as mentioned earlier in the example of Virtual Barry. Preserving oneself or being preserved by someone else may affect both the dying person's peace of mind and the well-being of the bereaved. Furthermore, it is not clear whether the possibility of digital afterlife and the use of digital media alters thoughts about the mind–body connection, and whether interaction with a person's digital afterlife alters one's spiritual journey through grief. Distinguishing between those that preserve their own or another's digital afterlife, those that mediate the experience of others and those that receive the digital afterlife of a deceased person is important when considering the intended and unintended consequences of the very existence of digital afterlives.

ROBOT CARING

Using robots for caring and supporting humans offers people opportunities to connect with something emotionally and feel supported, even loved, without the need to reciprocate. It is likely that such intimacy will develop in the near future as there is customer demand for this, particularly in countries such as Japan. For example, Kolstad et al. (2020) examined the process of integrating assistive robots into Japanese nursing care in 2019. The study sought to evaluate the use of robots from the perspective of and response from elderly, people and nursing staff. As yet there has been no debate about the death of robots and indeed if this needs to be considered, nor has there been any discussion about the use of robots for the care of the dying, in for example hospice settings. An issue of concern is that of intimacy ethics, particularly if robots are used to care for the dying.

DIGITAL BURIAL

Whilst as yet there is little research in this area, it is likely that there will come a point when people decided to bury their dead digitally. This may be in the form of deleting Facebook profiles and memorial pages or stored phone messages. Alternatively, it might be in the form of disregarding the dead, where instead of actively deleting the social media profiles and digital data, these are ignored, left behind and put away. Digital burial is therefore defined here as deleting, hiding or ignoring loved one's digital media in order to refocus on integrating the dead into their life, rather than constantly returning to the dead to speak to them as if they were there. Digital burial offers the living the opportunity to grow around the grief instead of feeling dominated by the ongoing media presence of the dead. Examples of digital burial include areas such as deletion, the complete deletion, and therefore, burial of all social networking sites, digital photographs and music, and partial deletion where some artefacts and legacies are deleted and others are not; digital memorialization where all social networking sites are deleted but a private online memorial site is created; and pre-death digital burial where the person can opt to have their social media accounts deleted upon their death.

It is clear from this discussion that artificial intelligence, death and dying issues still require considerable exploration, legal guidance and in-depth research.

REFLECTION AND CONCLUSION

There is a sense now that media death and death in digital spaces at times are taking on a larger reality than everyday life – the virtual has become the real so that 'rather than art imitating life, life imitates art. One's social currency begins to feel *real* and the importance of presence becomes neglected' (Cann, 2014: 76). Thus, replication occurs in digital spaces through symbols such as crosses, angels and memes, as well as poems and maxims. The physical images of death are transposed onto digital platforms. The result is that the reproduction of memories, photographs and occasions on social media does appear as if the image 'being repeated no longer refers to things themselves but to their reproductions' (Foucault, 1987: 22). It is as if death and death memories are being reproduced and replicated all the time, constantly all over the world in an end-less cycle of replication. This re-fabrication results in diverse perspectives, copies, performances, enactments and artefacts. Life and death issues merge in digital spaces and often result in the feeling of living with the liminal, dwelling on the oblique and residing on the edges of the end.

REFERENCES

AlgorithmWatch (2019). In cooperation with Bertelsmann Stiftung. Automating Society – Taking Stock of Automated Decision-Making in the EU. www.algorithmwatch.org/automating-society/.

Alves, R. V. (2021). The Internet, social media and grieving. *Médecine Palliative*. doi:10.1016/j.medpal.2020.04.006.

Andrejevic, M. (2002). The work of being watched: Interactive media and the exploitation of self-disclosure. *Critical Studies in Media Communication, 19*(2), 230–248.

Aubuchon, R., & Moore, R. D. (Creators). (2010). *Caprica* [TV Series]. New York: Syf.

Bainbridge, W. (2013). Perspectives on virtual veneration. *Information Society, 29* (3), 196–202.

Bainbridge, W. (2017). The virtual conquest of death. In M. H. Jacobsen, (Ed.). *Postmortal Society – Towards a Sociology of Immortality*. London: Routledge.

Ball, A. (2001–2005). *Six Feet Under*. Los Angeles, CA: Warner Bros.

Barron, C. (2003). A strong distinction between humans and non-humans is no longer required for research purposes: A debate between Bruno Latour and Steve Fuller. *History of the Human Sciences, 16*(2), 77–99.

Bassett, D. (2018). Digital afterlives: From social media platforms to thanabots and beyond. In: C. Tandy, (Ed.), *Death and Anti-Death, Vol. 16: 200 Years After Frankenstein*. Ann Arbor, MI: Ria UP.

Bassett, D. (2020). Profit and loss – The mortality of the digital immortality platforms. In M. Savin-Baden, & V. Mason-Robbie (Eds.), *Digital Afterlife. Death Matters in a Digital Age*. Boca Raton, FL: CRC Press.

Bell, G., & Gray, J. (2000). 'Digital Immortality'. Technical report for Microsoft Research. Available online https://www.microsoft.com/en-us/research/wp-content/uploads/2016/02/tr-2000-101.pdf.

Benford, S., Bowers, J., Fahl´en, L., Greenhalgh, C., & Snowdon, D. (1995). User embodiment in collaborative virtual environments. In *Proceedings of ACM Conference on Human Factors in Computing Systems*. New York: ACM Press.

Berman, R. (1995). *Star Trek: Voyager [TV series]*. Los Angeles, CA: CBS Television.

Big Brother Watch (2019). FaceOff. https://bigbrotherwatch.org.uk/campaigns/stop-facial-recognition/.

Borenstein, J., & Arkin, R. C. (2016). Robots, ethics, and intimacy: The need for scientific research. In: Conference of the International Association for Computing and Philosophy (IACAP 2016). Ferrara, IT, June.

Brandtzæg, P. B., Lüders, M., & Skjetne, J. H. (2010). Too many Facebook "friends"? Content sharing and sociability versus the need for privacy in social network sites. *Journal of Human-Computer Interaction*, *26*(11–12), 1006–1030.

Brooker, C., & Harris, O. (2013). Be Right Back. Black Mirror [TV Episode]. Westminster, UK: Channel 4.

Brubaker, J. R., Hayes, G. R., & Mazmanian, M. (2019). Orienting to networked grief: Situated perspectives of communal mourning on facebook. In Proceedings of the ACM on Human-Computer Interaction 3, CSCW, Article 27 (November 2019), 19 pages. doi:10.1145/3359129Brubaker.

Burden, D. J. H. (2012). *Digital Immortality*. Presentation at Birmingham, UK: TEDx.

Burden, D. (2020). Building a digital immortal. In M. Savin-Baden, & V. Mason-Robbie (Eds.), *Digital Afterlife. Death Matters in a Digital Age*. Boca Raton, FL: CRC Press.

Burden, D., & Savin-Baden, M. (2019). *Virtual Humans: Today and Tomorrow*. Boca Raton, FL: CRC Press.

Burden, D. J. H., Savin-Baden, M., & Bhakta, R. (2016). Covert implementations of the Turing test: A more level playing field? In International Conference on Innovative Techniques and Applications of Artificial Intelligence (pp. 195–207). Cham, Switzerland: Springer.

Buben, A. (2015). Technology of the dead: Objects of loving remembrance or replaceable resources? *Philosophical Papers, 44* (1), 15–37. doi:10.1080/05568641.2015.1014538.

Cadwalladr, C. (2014). Are the robots about to rise? Google's new director of engineering thinks so .... Available online http://www.theguardian.com/technology/2014/feb/22/robots-google-ray-kurzweil-terminator-singularity-artificial-intelligence

Call of Duty [computer software]. (2003–2020). Santa Monica, CA: Activision.

Camus, A. (1942a). *L'Entranger.* Paris: Gallimard.

Camus, A. (1942b). *Le Mythe de Sisyphe.* Paris: Gallimard.

Cann, C. (2014). Tweeting death, posting photos, and pinning memorials: Remembering the dead in bits and pieces. In C. M. Moreman, & A. D. Lewis (Eds.), *Digital Death Mortality and Beyond in the Online Age.* Satn Barbara, CA: Praeger.

Cann, C. (2018). Buying an Afterlife: mapping religious beliefs through consumer death goods. In C. Cann (Ed.), *The Routledge Handbook of Death and Afterlife* (pp. 377–392). Oxford: Routledge.

Celestis. (n.d.). Fulfilling the dreams of a lifetime. Celestis Memorial Spaceflights. Available online https://www.celestis.com/.

Clabburn, O., Groves, K. E., & Jack, B. (2020) Virtual learning environment ('Ivy Street') for palliative medicine education: Student and facilitator evaluation. *BMJ Supportive & Palliative Care, 10,* 318–323.

Clarke, J. N. (2006). Death under control: The portrayal of death in mass print english language magazines in Canada. *OMEGA, 52* (2), 153–167.

Collins, B. (2021). Microsoft Could Bring You Back From The Dead... As A Chat Bot Forbes Jan 4, Available online https://www.forbes.com/sites/barrycollins/2021/01/04/microsoft-could-bring-you-back-from-the-dead-as-a-chat-bot/.

Cook, S. L. (2007). Funerary practices and afterlife expectations in ancient Israel. *Religion Compass, 1*(6), 660–683.

Cook, D. M., Dissanayake, D. N., & Kaur, K. (2019). The usability factors of lost digital legacy data from regulatory misconduct: Older values and the issue of ownership. In 2019 7th International Conference on Information and Communication Technology (ICoICT) (pp. 1–6).

Data Protection Act (2018). c. 12 Available online http://www.legislation.gov.uk/ukpga/2018/12/contents/enacted.

Davies, J. D. (2008). *The Theology of Death*. London: Continuum.

De Abaitua, M. (2009). *The Red Men*. London: Snowbooks Ltd.

DeAtley, T. (2020). Grief by the byte: Constructions of data consent, privacy, and stability in griefbots. In J. Grandinetti, T. DeAtley, & J. Bruinsma (Eds.), *The Dead Speak: Big Data and Digitally Mediated Death. Panel Presented At Aoir 2020: The 21th Annual Conference of the Association of Internet Researchers*. Virtual Event: AoIR. Available online http://spir.aoir.org.

Deeley, M. (Producer) & Scott, R. (Director), (1982). *Blade Runner* [Motion Picture]. Burbank, CA: Warner Bros.

DeGroot, J. M. (2014). 'For whom the bell tolls': Emotional rubbernecking in Facebook memorial groups. *Death Studies*, 38(2), 79–84. doi:10.1080/07481187.2012.725450.

Dennett, D. C. (1995). The unimagined preposterousness of zombies. *Journal of Consciousness Studies*, 2(4), 322–326.

Docherty, B. (2016). Losing control: The dangers of killer robots. *The Conversation*, June 16th, 2016.

Doherty, G., Firth, C., Lancaster, D. (Producers) & Hood, G. (Director), (2015). Eye in the Sky [Motion Picture] United Kingdom: Entertainment One Films.

Doka, K. J. (2008). Disenfranchised grief in historical and cultural perspective. In M. S. Stroebe, R. O. Hansson, H. Schut, & W. Stroebe (Eds.), *Handbook of Bereavement Research and Practice: Advances in Theory and Intervention* (pp. 223–240). American Psychological Association. doi:10.1037/14498-011.

Dubbin, R. (2013). The rise of twitter bots. The New Yorker. Available online http://www.newyorker.com/tech/elements/the-rise-of-twitter-bots.du Preez, A. (2018). Sublime selfies: To witness death. *European Journal of Cultural Studies*, 21(6), 744–760.

Durkheim, E. (2001/1912). *The Elementary Forms of Religious Life.* (C. Cosman, Trans.). Oxford: Oxford University Press.

Eliot, T. S. (1942). *Little Gidding, The Four Quartets.* London: Faber and Faber.

Estep, E. (2013). 7 Powerful Ways to Maintain Your Privacy and Integrity Online. Available online http://www.collective-evolution.com/2013/06/13/7-powerful-ways-to-maintain-your-privacy-and-integrity-online/.

Feige, K. (Producer) & Whedon, J. (Directors) (2015). *Avengers: Age of Ultron* [Motion Picture]. Burbank, CA: Marvel Studios.

Fiegerman, S. (2013). Netflix's Data Points Are Not the Usual Suspects. Available online https://mashable.com/2013/12/11/netflix-data/.

Field, N. P. (2006). Unresolved grief and continuing bonds: An attachment perspective. *Death Studies, 30,* 739–756. doi:10.1080/07481180600850518.

Fitzpatrick, K. K., Darcy, A., & Vierhile, M. (2017). Delivering cognitive behavior therapy to young adults with symptoms of depression and anxiety using a fully automated conversational agent (Woebot): A randomized controlled trial. *The Journal of Medical Internet Research Mental Health, 4*(2), e19. doi:10.2196/mental.7785.

Floridi, L. (2014). *The Fourth Revolution—How the Infosphere is Reshaping Human Reality.* Oxford: Oxford University Press.

Foucault, M. (1987). *Death and the Labyrinth: The World of Raymond Roussel,* trans. C. Ruas London: Athlone Press.

Froese T., & Ziemke T. (2009). Enactive artificial intelligence: Investigating the systemic organization of life and mind. *Artificial Intelligence, 173*(3–4), 466–500.

Frude, N., & Jandric, P. (2015). The Intimate Machine – 30 years on. *E-Learning and Digital Media, 12*(3–4), 410–424.

Fuller, S., & Jandrić, P. (2019). The postdigital human: Making the history of the future. *Postdigital Science and Education, 1*(1), 190–217. doi:10.1007/s42438-018-0003-x.

Garland, A. (2020). Devs [TV Series].

Gehl, J. (2000). CyberAll: Everywhere and forever, an interview with Gordon Bell. *Ubiquity,* Issue May, doi:10.1145/341836.341837. Available online http://ubiquity.acm.org/article.cfm?id=341837

Gervacio, J. (2019). Cyber-Mourning: Toward a Psychological Understanding of Grief on Social Media. *ETD Collection for Pace University*. AAI13916001. https://digitalcommons.pace.edu/dissertations/AAI13916001.

Giaxoglou, K. (2020). Mobilizing grief and remembrance with and for networked publics: towards a typology of hyper-mourning. *European Journal of Life Writing*, Vol IX, 264–284 2020. doi:10.21827/ejlw.9.36910

Gibbs, S. (2016). Chatbot lawyer overturns 160,000 parking tickets in London and New York. The Guardian. Available online https://www.theguardian.com/technology/2016/jun/28/chatbot-ai-lawyer-donotpayparking-tickets-london-new-york.

Giddens, A. (1991). *Modernity and Self-Identity*. Oxford: Polity.

Giles, J. (2010). Cyber crime made easy. *New Scientist*, 205(2752), 20–21.

Gillespie, A., & Corti, K. (2016). The body that speaks: Recombining bodies and speech sources in unscripted face-to-face communication. *Frontiers in Psychology*, 7, 1300. Available online https://www.frontiersin.org/articles/10.3389/fpsyg.2016.01300/full.

Godfrey (2018). The Griefbot that could change how we mourn. Daily Beast. https://www. thedailybeast.com/the-griefbot-that-could-change-how-we-mourn.

Gomes de Andrade, N., Pawson, D., Muriello, D., et al. (2018). Ethics and artificial intelligence: Suicide prevention on Facebook. *Philosophy & Technology*, 31, 669–684. doi:10.1007/s13347-018-0336-0.

Gooder, P. (2011). *Heaven*. London: SPCK Publishing.

Grandinetti, J. (2020). Reaminator: Haunted data, streaming media, and subjectivity. In J. Grandinetti, T. DeAtley, & J. Bruinsma (Eds.), *The dead speak: Big Data and Digitally Mediated Death. Panel Presented At Aoir 2020: The 21th Annual Conference of the Association of Internet Researchers. Virtual Event: AoIR*. Available online http://spir.aoir.org.

Haeker. R. (2019). Artificial intelligence in the image of God? Available online https://williamtemplefoundation.org.uk/blog-artificial-intelligence-in-the-image-of-god/.

Hakola, O. (2013) Normal death on television: Balancing privacy and voyeurism. *Thanatos, 2* (2), 56–71.

Hanson, R. (2008). Economics of the Singularity. IEEE Spectrum. Available online electronically at http://spectrum.ieee.org/robotics/robotics-software/economics-of-the-singularity.

Haraway, D. ([1985] 1991). *Simians, Cyborgs, and Women: The Reinvention of Nature*. New York: Routledge.

Harbinja, E. (2017a). *Legal Aspects of Transmission of Digital Assets on Death* (Unpublished PhD thesis). University of Strathclyde.

Harbinja, E. (2017b). Post-mortem privacy 2.0: Theory, law, and technology. *International Review of Law, Computers & Technology, 31*(1), 26–42. doi:10.1080/13600869.2017.1275116.

Harbinja, E. (2020). The 'new(ish)' property, informational bodies and postmortality. In M. Savin-Baden, & V. Mason-Robbie (Eds.), *Digital Afterlife. Death Matters in a Digital Age*. Boca Raton, FL: CRC Press.

Hayes, S. (2021). The value of postdigital humans as objects, or subjects, in McDonaldised Society. In M. Savin-Baden, (Ed.), *Postdigital Humans*. London: Springer.

Hayles, K. (1999). *How We Became Posthuman: Virtual Bodies in Cybernetics, Literature and Informatics*. Chicago, IL: University of Chicago Press.

Hayles, N. K. (2012). *How We Think: Digital Media and Contemporary Technogenesis*. Chicago, IL: University of Chicago Press.

Hayter, D. (2000). *X-Men*. Los Angeles, California: 20th Century FoxHayward, D. B., Fellner, E., & Hooper, T. (Producers) Hooper, T. (Director) (2019). *Cats* [Motion picture]. London, UK: Universal Pictures.

Heidegger, M. (Trans). (1971). *The Thing* in Poetry, Language, Thought (A. Hofstader, Trans.). New York: HarperCollins Publishers Inc.

Hern, A. (2017). 'Give robots "personhood" status, EU committee argues' *The Guardian* 17th January.

Herzfeld, N. (2002). Creating in our own image: Artificial intelligence and the image of god. *Journal of Religion and Science, 37* (2), 303–316.

Hertz, R. (1960). *Death and the Right Hand*. (R. Needham & C. Needham, Trans.). Glencoe, IL: Free Press.

House of Lords Select Committee, AI in the UK: ready, willing and able? (April 2018) Available online https://publications.parliament.uk/pa/ld201719/ldselect/ldai/100/10002.html.

Hunter, C. (2018). *The After Wife*. London: Trapeze.

Hutchings, T. (2010). Creating Church Online: An Ethnographic Study of Five Internet-Based Christian Communities (PhD thesis, Durham University).

Hyatt, B. (2009). There Is NO Virtual Church (Part One) (2009). Available online http://www.christianitytoday.com/pastors/2009/august-online-only/there-is-no-virtual-church-part-1.html.

Ingraham, C., & Rowland, A. (2016). Performing imperceptibility: Google street view and the tableau vivant. *Surveillance & Society*, *14*(2), 211–226.

Irwin, M. D. (2015). Mourning 2.0—Continuing bonds between the living and the dead on Facebook. *Omega: Journal of Death and Dying*, *72*(2), 119–150. doi:10.1177/0030222815574830.

Ito, M., Baumer, S., Bittanti, M., Boyd, D., Cody, R., Herr-Stephenson, B., et al. (2010). *Hanging Out, Messing Around, and Geeking Out*. Cambridge, MA: MIT Press.

Jaafar, N. I., Darmawan, B., & Mohamed Ariffin, M. Y. (2014). 'Face-to-face or not-to-face: A technology preference for communication', *Cyberpsychology, Behavior and Social Networking, 17*(11), 702–708. doi:10.1089/cyber.2014.0098.

Jandrić, P. (2020). Postdigital afterlife: A philosophical framework. In M. Savin-Baden, & V. Mason-Robbie (Eds.), *Digital Afterlife. Death Matters in a Digital Age*. Boca Raton, FL: CRC Press.

Jandrić, P., Knox, J., Besley, T., Ryberg, T., Suoranta, J., & Hayes, S. (2018). Postdigital science and education. *Educational Philosophy and Theory*, *50*(10), 893–899. doi:10.1080/00131857.2018.1454000.

Jones, B. (2020). The influence of social media on murder. *Electronic Theses, Projects, and Dissertations, 1123*. Available online https://scholarworks.lib.csusb.edu/etd/1123.

Jones, C. (2018). Experience and networked learning. In N. Bonderup Dohn, S. Cranmer, J. A. Sime, M. de Laat, & T. Ryberg (Eds.), *Networked Learning: Reflections and Challenges* (pp. 39–55). Springer International. doi:10.1007/978-3-319-74857-3_3.

Kant, I. (1998). *Grundlegung zur Metaphysik der Sitten*, translated and edited by M. Gregor, *Groundwork of the Metaphysics of Morals*. Cambridge: Cambridge University Press.

Karsoho, H. (2015). The Supreme court of Canada ruling in Carter v. Canada: A new era of end-of-life care for Canadians. *Bioethique Online, 4,* 1e3. http://bioethiqueonline.ca/4/4.

Karsosho, H., Fishman, J. R., Wright, D. K., & Macdonald, D. E. (2016). Suffering and medicalization at the end of life: The case of physician assisted dying. *Social Science & Medicine, 170,* 188–196.

Kasket, E. (2012). Continuing bonds in the age of social networking: Facebook as a modern-day medium. *Bereavement Care, 31* (2), 62–69.

Kasket, E. (2019). *All the Ghosts in the Machine: Illusions of Immortality in the Digital Age*. London, UK: Robinson.

Kasket, E. (2021). If death is the spectacle, big teach is the lens: How social media frame an age of 'spectacular death' In M. H. Jacobsen (Ed.), *The Age of Spectacular Death*. Oxford: Routledge.

Kastenbaum, R. J. (2004). *Death, Society, and Human Experience* (8th Edition). Boston: Allyn & Bacon.

Kitchin, R. (2014). *The Data Revolution: Big Data, Open Data, Data Infrastructures and Their Consequences*. London: Sage.

Kitchin, R., & McArdle, G. (2016). What makes Big Data, Big Data? Exploring the ontological characteristics of 26 datasets. *Big Data and Society, 3*(1), 1–12.

Klass, D. (2006). Continuing conversation about continuing bonds. *Death Studies, 30*(9), 843–858. doi:10.1080/07481180600886959.

Klass, D. (2018). Prologue. In D. Klass, & E. M. Steffen (Eds.), *Continuing Bonds in Bereavement: New Directions for Research and Practice* (pp. xiii–xix). New York: Routledge.

Klass, D., Silverman, P. R., & Nickman, S. L. (Eds.) (1996). *Continuing Bonds: New Understandings of Grief*. Washington, DC: Taylor & Francis.

Kocaballi, A. B., Berkovsky, S., Quiroz, J. C., Laranjo, L., Tong, H. L., Rezazadegan, D., & Coiera, E. (2019). 'The personalization of conversational agents in health care: Systematic review. *Journal of Medical Internet Research, 21*(11), e15360.

Koktan, S. (2017). Death 2.0: Facebook Memorial Pages. Technical Communication Capstone Course. 15. Minnesota State

University Mankato. Retrieved from https://cornerstone.lib.mnsu. edu/eng_tech_comm_capstone_course/15/.

Kolstad, M., Yamaguchi, N., Babic, A., & Nishihara Y. (2020). Integrating socially assistive robots into Japanese nursing care. *Studies in Health Technology and Informatics, 270,* 1323–1324. doi:10.3233/ SHTI200423. PMID: 32570640.

Kosove, A., et al. (Producers). & Villeneuve, D. (Director), (2017). *Blade Runner 2049* [Motion Picture]. Burbank, CA: Warner Bros.

Kosove, A. A., Johnson, B., Cohen, K., Polvino, M., Marter, A., Valder, D., Ryder, A. (Producers) & Pfister, W. (Director) (2014). *Transcendence.* [Motion Picture]. Burbank, CA: Warner Bros.

Kubler-Ross, E. (1969). *On Death and Dying.* London: Macmillan.

Kubrick, S. (Director & Producer & Screenplay), & Clarke, A. C. (Screenplay) (1968). 2001: *A Space Odyssey* [Motion picture]. Los Angeles, CA: Metro-Goldwyn-Mayer.

Landström, M., & Mustafa, N. (2018). Developing an Artificially Intelligent Tool for Grief Recovery. Master of Science Thesis MMK 2017: 172 IDE 304. Available online http://www.diva-portal.org/smash/ get/diva2:1211163/FULLTEXT01.pdf.

Leviathan, Y. (2018). Google Duplex: An AI System for Accomplishing Real-World Tasks Over the Phone on *Google AI Blog.* Available online https://ai.googleblog.com/2018/05/duplex-ai-system-for-natural-conversation.html.

Levy, D. (2008). *Love and Sex with Robots: The Evolution of Human-Robot Relationships.* New York: Harper Perennial.

Lipp, S. N., & O'Brien, K. M. (2020). Bereaved college students: Social support, coping style, continuing bonds, and social media use as predictors of complicated grief and posttraumatic growth. *Omega.* doi:10.1177/0030222820941952.

Lu, D. (2019). AI can predict if you'll die soon – but we've no idea how it works. *New Scientist,* November. Available online https://www. newscientist.com/article/2222907-ai-can-predict-if-youll-die-soon-but-weve-no-idea-how-it-works/.

Lynn, C., & Rath, A. (2012). GriefNet: Creating and Maintaining an Internet Bereavement Community. In C. Sofka, I. N. Cupit & K. R.

Gilbert (Eds.), *Dying, Death and Grief in an Online Universe*. New York: Springer.

Lyon, D. (2010). Liquid surveillance: The contribution of zygmunt bauman to surveillance studies. *International Political Sociology, 14*, 325–338.

Macdonald, A. (Producer). Garland, A. (Writer & Director) (2015). *Ex Machina* [Motion picture]. London, UK: Universal Pictures.

McDannell, C., & Lang, B. (2001). *Heaven – A History*. New Haven, CT: Yale University Press.

McDonald, I. (2006). *River of Gods*. Amherst, MA: Pyr.

McGrath, J. F. (2011). Robots, Rights Robots, Rights and Religion. Available online https://digitalcommons.butler.edu/cgi/viewcontent.cgi?article=1198&context=facsch_papers.

Maciel, C. (2011). Issues of the social web interaction project faced with afterlife digital legacy. In *Proceedings of the 10th Brazilian Symposium on Human Factors in Computing Systems and the 5th Latin American Conference on Human-Computer Interaction* (pp. 3–12). ACM Press.

Maciel, C., & Pereira, V. (2013). *Digital Legacy and Interaction*. Heidelberg: Springer.

Malle, B. F. (2016). Integrating robot ethics and machine morality: The study and design of moral competence in robots. *Ethics Information Technology, 18*, 243–256.

Martine, A. (2019). *A Memory Called Empire*. New York: Macmillan.

Mason-Robbie, V. (2021). Experience of using a virtual life coach: A case study of novice users. In: M. Savin-Baden (Ed.), *Postdigital Humans*. London: Springer.

Massimi, M., & Charise, A. (2009). Dying, death, and mortality: Towards thanatosensitivity in HCI. In *Proceedings of the Extended Abstracts of Conference on Human Factors in Computing Systems (CHI 2009)* (pp. 2459–2468). ACM Press.

Michel, A. H. (2013). Interview: The professor of robot love. Center for the Study of the Drone, October 5. Available online http://drone-center.bard.edu/interview-professor-robot-love/.

Moggach L. (2014). *Kiss Me First*. London: Picador.

Moncur, E., van den Hoven, E., Julius, M., & Kirk, D. (2015). Story shell: The participatory design of a bespoke digital memorial. In *Proceedings of the 4th Participatory Innovation Conference 2015* (pp. 470–477). The Hague: Hague University of Applied Science.

Moore, J., Magee, S., Gamreklidze, E., & Kowalewski, J. (2019). Social media mourning: Using grounded theory to explore how people grieve on social networking sites. *Omega (Westport)*, *79*(3), 231–259. doi:10.1177/0030222817709691.

Mori, M. (1970). The uncanny valley. *Energy, 7*(4), 33–35.Morse, T., & Birnhack. M. (2020). Digital Remains: The users' perspectives. In M. Savin-Baden, & V. Mason-Robbie (Eds.), *Digital Afterlife. Death Matters in a Digital Age*. Boca Raton, FL: CRC Press.

Moss, M. (2004). Grief on the web. *Omega: Journal of Death and Dying, 49*, 77–81.

Murray-Parkes, C. (1971). 'Psycho-social transitions: A field for study', *Social Science and Medicine, 5*(2), 101–115.

Nakamura, L. (2010). Race and identity in digital media. In J. Curran (Ed.), *Mass Media and Society*. London, UK: Bloomsbury Academic.

Nansen, B., Arnold, M., Gibbs, M., & Kohn, T. (2015). The Restless dead in the digital cemetery, digital death: Mortality and beyond in the online age. In C. M. Moreman, & A. D. Lewis (Eds.), *Digital Death: Mortality and Beyond in the Online Age* (pp. 111–124). Santa Barbara: Praeger.

Newton, C. (2016, October 6). Speak, Memory. Available online https://www.theverge.com/a/luka-artificial-intelligence-memorial-roman-mazurenko-bot.

Odom, W., Harper, R., Sellen, A., Kirk, D., & Banks, R. (2010). Passing on & Putting to rest: Understanding bereavement in the context of interactive technologies. In *Proceedings of SIGCHI Conference on Human Factors in Computing Systems* (pp. 1831–1840), CHI '10. Atlanta, USA. ACM Press.

Odom, W., Uriu, D., Kirk, D., Banks, R., & Wakkary, R. (2018). Experiences in designing technologies for honoring deceased loved ones. *Design Issues, 34* (1), 54–66.

Öhman, C. J., Gorwa, R., & Floridi, L. (2019). Prayer-bots and religious worship on twitter: A Call for a wider research Agenda. *Minds & Machines, 29*, 331–338. doi:10.1007/s11023-019-09498-3.

Oliver, D. P., Washington, K. T., Wittenberg-Lyles, E., Demiris, G., & Porock D. (2009). 'They're part of the team': Participant evaluation of the ACTIVE intervention. *Palliative Medicine, 23* (6), 549–55.

Otrel-Cass, K., & Fasching, M. (2021). Postdigital truths: Educational reflections on fake news and digital identities. In M. Savin-Baden, (Ed.), *Postdigital Humans*. London: Springer.

Perfect Choice Funerals. (2020). 70% of over 50s are unaware that social media accounts can be memorialised, leaving thousands of 'ghost' profiles active. Available online https://www.funeralplans.co.uk/in-the-news/70-of-over-50s-unaware-that-social-media-accounts-can-be-memorialised/.

Pitsillides, P. (2019). Digital legacy: Designing with things. *Death Studies, 43*(7), 426–434. doi:10.1080/07481187.2018.1541939.

Prigerson, H., Frank, E., Kasl, S., Reynolds, C., Anderson, B., Zubenko, G., Houck, P., George, C., & Kupfer, D. (1995). Complicated grief and bereavement-related depression as distinct disorders: Preliminary empirical validation in elderly bereaved spouses. *American Journal of Psychiatry, 2*, 1–12.

Prinz, J. J. (2011). Is empathy necessary for morality? In A. Coplan, & P. Goldie (Eds.), *Empathy: Philosophical and Psychological Perspectives* (pp. 211–229). Oxford: Oxford University Press.

Prisco, G. (2018). *Tales of the Turing Church: Hacking Religion, Enlightening Science, Awakening Technology*. Independently Published.

Rappaport Z.H. (2006) Robotics and artificial intelligence: Jewish ethical perspectives. In: Nimsky C., Fahlbusch R. (eds) Medical Technologies in Neurosurgery. *Acta Neurochirurgica Supplements*, vol 98. Springer, Vienna. doi: 10.1007/978-3-211-33303-7_2

Recchia, G. (2020). The fall and rise of AI: Investigating AI narratives with computational methods. In S. Dillon, S. Cave, & K. Dihal (Eds.), *AI Narratives: A History of Imaginative Thinking about Intelligent Machines*. Oxford: Oxford University Press.

Reed, R. (2019). AI in Religion, AI for Religion, AI and Religion: Towards a theory of Religious Studies and Artificial Intelligence. American Academy of Religion, Annual Meeting. Available online https://www.academia.edu/download/61113530/Toward_a_Theory_of_Religion_and_A.I.pdf.

Rhodan, M. (2015). This advocacy group is saying 'Hell No' to 'Hello Barbie'. Time. Available online http://time.com/4093660/barbie-hell-no/.

Riek, L. D., & Howard, D. (2014). A Code of Ethics for the Human-Robot Interaction Profession (April 4). Proceedings of we Robot, 2014. Available online SSRN: https://ssrn.com/abstract=2757805.

Ritzer, G. (1993/2018). *The McDonaldisation of Society: Into the Digital Age* (9th ed.). Thousand Oaks, CA: Sage Publications.

Robertson, J. (2010). Gendering humanoid robots: Robo-sexism in Japan. *Body & Society*, *16*(2), 1–36.

Rossetto, K. R., Lannutti, P. J., & Strauman, E. C. (2015). Death on Facebook: Examining the roles of social media communication for the bereaved. *Journal of Social and Personal Relationships*, *32*(7), 974–994.

Rycroft, G. (2020). Legal issues in digital afterlife. In M. Savin-Baden, & V. Mason-Robbie (Eds.), *Digital Afterlife. Death Matters in a Digital Age*. Boca Raton, FL: CRC Press.

Saltzman, M. (2018). How to see everything Netflix knows about you. Retrieved from https://www.usatoday.com/story/tech/columnist/saltzman/2018/04/17/you-can-see-whatnetflix-knows-you-but-you-cant-download/510782002/.

Savin-Baden, M., & Bhakta, R. (2019). Problem-based learning in digital spaces. In M. Moallem, W. Hung, & N. Dabbagh (Eds.), *Wiley Handbook of Problem-Based Learning*. New York: Wiley.

Savin-Baden, M., & Burden, D. (2018). Digital immortality and virtual humans. *Journal of Post digital Science and Education*, *1*(1), 87–103.

Savin-Baden, M., & Falconer, L. (2016). Learning at the interstices; locating practical philosophies for understanding physical/virtual interspaces. *Interactive Learning Environments*, 24(5), 991–1003.

Savin-Baden, M., Burden, D., Bhakta, R., & Mason-Robbie, V. (2019). An evaluation of the effectiveness of using pedagogical agents for teaching in inclusive ways. In Y. Wang, M. Gallagher, & J. Knox (Eds.), *Speculative Futures for Artificial Intelligence and Educational Inclusion*. London: Springer.

Savin-Baden, M., Burden, D., & Taylor, H. (2017). The ethics and impact of digital immortality. Special Issue of *Knowledge Cultures - Technologies and Time in the Age of Global Neoliberal Capitalism*, *5*(2) 11–29.

Savin-Baden, M., Tombs, G., Burden, D., & Wood, C. (2013). 'It's almost like talking to a person': Student disclosure to pedagogical agents in sensitive settings. *International Journal of Mobile and Blended Learning, 5*(2), 78–93.

Schroeder, N. L., & Adesope, O. O. (2014). A systematic review of pedagogical agents' persona, motivation, and cognitive load implications for learners. *Journal of Research on Technology in Education, 46*(3), 229–251.

Schuurman, D. C. (2019). Artificial intelligence: Discerning a Christian response. *Perspectives on Science & Christian Faith, 71* (2), 75–82.

Schweitzer, A. (1907/1974). Overcoming Death *Reverence for Life*. London: SPCK, pp. 67–81.

Sebold, A. (2003). *The Lovely Bones*. London: Picador.

Shakespeare, W. (1590/2002). *A Midsummer Night's Dream*. In The Complete Pelican Shakespeare. London: Penguin.

Shakespeare, W. (1609/2008). *Hamlet* (Reissue edition.). Oxford: OUP.

Shakespeare, W. (1633/2008). *The Tragedy of King Richard III* (1st ed.). The Oxford Shakespeare. Oxford: OUP.

Shusterman, N. (2016). *Scythe*. New York: Simon & Schuster.

Singler, B. (2020). "Blessed by the algorithm": Theistic conceptions of artificial intelligence in online discourse. *AI & Society*. Available online https://www.researchgate.net/publication/341053764_Blessed_by_the_algorithm_Theistic_conceptions_of_artificial_intelligence_in_online_discourse.

Smartwood, R. M., McCarthy Veach, P., Kuhne, J., Lee, H. K., & Ji, K. (2011). Surviving grief: An analysis of the exchange of hope in online grief communities. *Omega: Journal of Death and Dying, 63*, 161–181.

Sofka, C. (2020). The transition from life to the digital afterlife: Thanatechnology and its impact on grief. In M. Savin-Baden, & V. Mason-Robbie (Eds.), *Digital Afterlife. Death Matters in a Digital Age*. Boca Raton, FL: CRC Press.

Stein, J. P., Appel, M., Jost, A., & Ohler, P. (2020). Matter over mind? How the acceptance of digital entities depends on their appearance, mental prowess, and the interaction between both. International Journal of Human-Computer Studies. Advance publication online. doi:10.1016/j.ijhcs.2020.102463.

Stokes, P. (2015). Deletion as second death: The moral status of digital remains. *Ethics and Information Technology, 17*(4), 237–248.

Stroebe, M., & Schut, H. (1999). The dual process model of coping with bereavement: Rationale and description. *Death Studies, 23*, 197–224.

Subramanian, H., Ramamoorthy, S., Stone, P., & Kuipers, B. J. (2006). Designing safe, profitable automated stock trading agents using evolutionary algorithms. In GECCO '06 *Proceedings of the 8th Annual Conference on Genetic and Evolutionary Computation, (GECCO'06)* (pp. 1777–1784). New York: ACM.

Tassinari, A., & Maccarone, V. (2020). Riders on the storm: Workplace solidarity among gig economy couriers in Italy and the UK. *Work Employment and Society, 34*(1), 35–54.

Taylor, L., Meyer, E. T. & Schroeder, R. (2014). Bigger and better, or more of the same? Emerging practices and perspectives on big data analysis in economics. *Big Data and Society.* July–December 1–10. doi:10.1177/2053951714536877.

Tonkin, L. (1996). Growing around grief—another way of looking at grief and recovery. *Bereavement Care, 15*(1), 10.

Turing, A. (1950). Computing machinery and intelligence. *Mind, 49*, 433–460.

Turkle, S. (2010). In good company? On the threshold of robotic companions. In Y. Wilks (Ed.), *Close Engagements with Artificial Companions: Key Social, Psychological, Ethical and Design Issues* (pp. 3–10), Amsterdam; Philadelphia, PA: John Benjamins.

Uriu, D., & Okude, N. (2010). ThanatoFenestra: Photographic family altar supporting a ritual to pray for the deceased. Paper presented at *Proceedings of the 8th ACM Conference on Designing Interactive Systems* (pp. 422–425). Aarhus, Denmark: ACM.

Villaronga, E. F. (2019). "I Love You," said the robot: Boundaries of the use of emotions in human-robot interactions. In Ayanoğlu, H., & Duarte, E. (Eds.) *Emotional Design in Human-Robot Interaction* (pp. 93–110). Cham: Springer.

Vincent, S., & Brackley, J. (2015). *Humans*. Channel 4 [TV Series].

Vinichenko, M. V., Chulanova, O. L., Vinogradova, M. V., & Amozova, L. N. (2020). The impact of artificial intelligence on society views of Islamic religious leaders. *European Journal of Science and Theology, 16*(3), 67–77.

Wachowski, A., & Wachowski, L. (1999). *The Matrix*. New York: Warner Bros.

Wagner, A. J. M. (2018). Do not Click "Like" When Somebody has Died: The Role of Norms for Mourning Practices in Social Media. *Social Media + Society*. doi:10.1177/2056305117744392.

Wallace, J., Montague, K., Duncan, T., Carvalho, L., Koulidou, N., Mahoney, J., Morrissey, K., Craig, C., Groot, L., Lawson, S., Olivier, P., Trueman, J., & Fisher, H. (2020). ReFind: design, lived experience and ongoingness in bereavement. In *CHI'20: Proceedings of the 2020 CHI Conference on Human Factors in Computing Systems*. New York: Association for Computing Machinery.

Walter, T. (1996). A new model of grief: Bereavement and biography. *Mortality, 1* (1), 7–25.

Walter, T., Hourizi, R., Moncur, W., & Pitsillides, S. (2012). Does the internet change how we die and mourn? Overview and analysis. *Omega: The Journal of Death and Dying, 64*(4), 275–302.

Weinstein, P., Rosenburg, M. (Producers) & Weir, P. (Director), (1993). *Fearless* [Motion Picture]. Burbank CA: Warner Bros.

Windisch, P., Hertler, C., Blum, D., Zwahlen, D., & Förster, R. (2020). Leveraging advances in artificial intelligence to improve the quality and timing of palliative care. *Cancers, 12* (5), 1149. doi:10.3390/cancers12051149.

Wiederhold B. K. (2019). Can artificial intelligence predict the end of life … and do we really want to know? *Cyberpsychology, Behaviour and Social Networks, 22* (5), 297–299.

Woodruf, A., Augustin, S., & Foucault, B. (2007). Sabbath day home automation: "It's like mixing technology and religion". In *CHI 2007*, April 28–May 3, 2007, San Jose, CA.

Žižek, S. (1999). The matrix, or two sides of perversion, Philosophy Today, 43. Online. http://www.nettime.org/Lists- Archives/nettime-l-9912/msg00019.html. Accessed 2 June 2014.

Zuboff, S. (2019). *The Age of Surveillance Capitalism: The Fight for a Human Future at the New Frontier of Power*. New York: PublicAffairs.

INDEX

Printed in the United States
by Baker & Taylor Publisher Services